Learning Big Data with Amazon Elastic MapReduce

Easily learn, build, and execute real-world Big Data
solutions using Hadoop and AWS EMR

Amarkant Singh

Vijay Rayapati

PUBLISHING

BIRMINGHAM - MUMBAI

Learning Big Data with Amazon Elastic MapReduce

First published: October 2014

Production reference: 1241014

Published by Packt Publishing Ltd.
Livery Place
35 Livery Street
Birmingham B3 2PB, UK.

ISBN 978-1-78217-343-4

www.packtpub.com

Cover image by Pratyush Mohanta (tysoncinematics@gmail.com)

Credits

About the Authors

Amarkant Singh is a Big Data specialist. Being one of the initial users of Amazon Elastic MapReduce, he has used it extensively to build and deploy many Big Data solutions. He has been working with Apache Hadoop and EMR for almost 4 years now. He is also a certified AWS Solutions Architect. As an engineer, he has designed and developed enterprise applications of various scales. He is currently leading the product development team at one of the most happening cloud-based enterprises in the Asia-Pacific region. He is also an all-time top user on Stack Overflow for EMR at the time of writing this book. He blogs at `http://www.bigdataspeak.com/` and is active on Twitter as `@singh_amarkant`.

Vijay Rayapati is the CEO of Minjar Cloud Solutions Pvt. Ltd., one of the leading providers of cloud and Big Data solutions on public cloud platforms. He has over 10 years of experience in building business rule engines, data analytics platforms, and real-time analysis systems used by many leading enterprises across the world, including Fortune 500 businesses. He has worked on various technologies such as LISP, .NET, Java, Python, and many NoSQL databases. He has rearchitected and led the initial development of a large-scale location intelligence and analytics platform using Hadoop and AWS EMR. He has worked with many ad networks, e-commerce, financial, and retail companies to help them design, implement, and scale their data analysis and BI platforms on the AWS Cloud. He is passionate about open source software, large-scale systems, and performance engineering. He is active on Twitter as `@amnigos`, he blogs at `amnigos.com`, and his GitHub profile is `https://github.com/amnigos`.

Acknowledgments

We would like to extend our gratitude to Udit Bhatia and Kartikeya Sinha from Minjar's Big Data team for their valuable feedback and support. We would also like to thank the reviewers and the Packt Publishing team for their guidance in improving our content.

About the Reviewers

Venkat Addala has been involved in research in the area of Computational Biology and Big Data Genomics for the past several years. Currently, he is working as a Computational Biologist in Positive Bioscience, Mumbai, India, which provides clinical DNA sequencing services (it is the first company to provide clinical DNA sequencing services in India). He understands Biology in terms of computers and solves the complex puzzle of the human genome Big Data analysis using Amazon Cloud. He is a certified MongoDB developer and has good knowledge of Shell, Python, and R. His passion lies in decoding the human genome into computer codecs. His areas of focus are cloud computing, HPC, mathematical modeling, machine learning, and natural language processing. His passion for computers and genomics keeps him going.

Vijay Raajaa G.S leads the Big Data / semantic-based knowledge discovery research with the Mu Sigma's Innovation & Development group. He previously worked with the BSS R&D division at Nokia Networks and interned with Ericsson Research Labs. He had architected and built a feedback-based sentiment engine and a scalable in-memory-based solution for a telecom analytics suite. He is passionate about Big Data, machine learning, Semantic Web, and natural language processing. He has an immense fascination for open source projects. He is currently researching on building a semantic-based personal assistant system using a multiagent framework. He holds a patent on churn prediction using the graph model and has authored a white paper that was presented at a conference on Advanced Data Mining and Applications. He can be connected at `https://www.linkedin.com/in/gsvijayraajaa`.

Gaurav Kumar has been working professionally since 2010 to provide solutions for distributed systems by using open source / Big Data technologies. He has hands-on experience in Hadoop, Pig, Hive, Flume, Sqoop, and NoSQLs such as Cassandra and MongoDB. He possesses knowledge of cloud technologies and has production experience of AWS.

His area of expertise includes developing large-scale distributed systems to analyze big sets of data. He has also worked on predictive analysis models and machine learning. He architected a solution to perform clickstream analysis for `Tradus.com`. He also played an instrumental role in providing distributed searching capabilities using Solr for `GulfNews.com` (one of UAE's most-viewed newspaper websites).

Learning new languages is not a barrier for Gaurav. He is particularly proficient in Java and Python, as well as frameworks such as Struts and Django. He has always been fascinated by the open source world and constantly gives back to the community on GitHub. He can be contacted at `https://www.linkedin.com/in/gauravkumar37` or on his blog at `http://technoturd.wordpress.com`. You can also follow him on Twitter `@_gauravkr`.

www.PacktPub.com

Support files, eBooks, discount offers, and more

You might want to visit www.PacktPub.com for support files and downloads related to your book.

Did you know that Packt offers eBook versions of every book published, with PDF and ePub files available? You can upgrade to the eBook version at www.PacktPub.com and as a print book customer, you are entitled to a discount on the eBook copy. Get in touch with us at service@packtpub.com for more details.

At www.PacktPub.com, you can also read a collection of free technical articles, sign up for a range of free newsletters and receive exclusive discounts and offers on Packt books and eBooks.

http://PacktLib.PacktPub.com

Do you need instant solutions to your IT questions? PacktLib is Packt's online digital book library. Here, you can access, read and search across Packt's entire library of books.

Why subscribe?

- Fully searchable across every book published by Packt
- Copy and paste, print and bookmark content
- On demand and accessible via web browser

Free access for Packt account holders

If you have an account with Packt at www.PacktPub.com, you can use this to access PacktLib today and view nine entirely free books. Simply use your login credentials for immediate access.

Instant updates on new Packt books

Get notified! Find out when new books are published by following @PacktEnterprise on Twitter, or the *Packt Enterprise* Facebook page.

I would like to dedicate this work, with love, to my parents Krishna Jiwan Singh and Sheela Singh, who taught me that in order to make dreams become a reality, it takes determination, dedication, and self-discipline. Thank you Mummy and Papaji.

Amarkant Singh

To my beloved parents, Laxmi Rayapati and Somaraju Rayapati, for their constant support and belief in me while I took all those risks.

I would like to thank my sister Sujata, my wife Sowjanya, and my brother Ravi Kumar for their guidance and criticism that made me a better person.

Vijay Rayapati

Table of Contents

Preface

It has been more than two decades since the Internet took the world by storm. Digitization has been gradually performed across most of the systems around the world, including the systems we have direct interfaces with, such as music, film, telephone, news, and e-shopping among others. It also includes most of the banking and government services systems.

We are generating enormous amount of digital data on a daily basis, which is approximately 2.5 quintillion bytes of data. The speed of data generation has picked up tremendously in the last few years, thanks to the spread of mobiles. Now, more than 75 percent of the total world population owns a mobile phone, each one of them generating digital data—not only when they connect to the Internet, but also when they make a call or send an SMS.

Other than the common sources of data generation such as social posts on Twitter and Facebook, digital pictures, videos, text messages, and thousands of daily news articles in various languages across the globe, there are various other avenues that are adding to the massive amount of data on a daily basis. Online e-commerce is booming now, even in the developing countries. GPS is being used throughout the world for navigation. Traffic situations are being predicted with better and better accuracy with each passing day.

All sorts of businesses now have an online presence. Over time, they have collected huge amount of data such as user data, usage data, and feedback data. Some of the leading businesses are generating huge amount of these kinds of data within minutes or hours. This data is what we nowadays very fondly like to call Big Data!

Technically speaking, any large and complex dataset for which it becomes difficult to store and analyze this data using traditional database or filesystems is called Big Data.

Processing of huge amounts of data in order to get useful information and actionable business insights is becoming more and more lucrative. The industry was well aware of the fruits of these huge data mines they had created. Finding out user behavior towards one's products can be an important input to drive one's business. For example, using historical data for cab bookings, it can be predicted (with good likelihood) where in the city and at what time a cab should be parked for better hire rates.

However, there was only so much they could do with the existing technology and infrastructure capabilities. Now, with the advances in distributed computing, problems whose solutions weren't feasible with single machine processing capabilities were now very much feasible. Various distributed algorithms came up that were designed to run on a number of interconnected computers. One such algorithm was developed as a platform by Doug Cutting and Mike Cafarella in 2005, named after Cutting's son's toy elephant. It is now a top-level Apache project called Apache Hadoop.

Processing Big Data requires massively parallel processing executing in tens, hundreds, or even thousands of clusters. Big enterprises such as Google and Apple were able to set up data centers that enable them to leverage the massive power of parallel computing, but smaller enterprises cannot even think of solving such Big Data problems yet.

Then came cloud computing. Technically, it is synonymous to distributed computing. Advances in commodity hardware, creation of simple cloud architectures, and community-driven open source software now bring Big Data processing within the reach of the smaller enterprises too. Processing Big Data is getting easier and affordable even for start-ups, who can simply rent processing time in the cloud instead of building their own server rooms.

Several players have emerged in the cloud computing arena. Leading among them is Amazon Web Services (AWS). Launched in 2006, AWS now has an array of software and platforms available for use as a service. One of them is Amazon Elastic MapReduce (EMR), which lets you spin-off a cluster of required size, process data, move the output to a data store, and then shut down the cluster. It's simple! Also, you pay only for the time you have the cluster up and running. For less than $10, one can process around 100 GB of data within an hour.

Advances in cloud computing and Big Data affect us more than we think. Many obvious and common features have been possible due to these technological enhancements in parallel computing. Recommended movies on Netflix, the *Items for you* sections in e-commerce websites, or the *People you may know* sections, all of these use Big Data solutions to bring these features to us.

With a bunch of very useful technologies at hand, the industry is now taking on its data mines with all their energy to mine the user behavior and predict their future actions. This enables businesses to provide their users with more personalized experiences. By knowing what a user might be interested in, a business may approach the user with a focused target—increasing the likelihood of a successful business.

As Big Data processing is becoming an integral part of IT processes throughout the industry, we are trying to introduce this Big Data processing world to you.

What this book covers

Chapter 1, Amazon Web Services, details how to create an account with AWS and navigate through the console, how to start/stop a machine on the cloud, and how to connect and interact with it. A very brief overview of all the major AWS services that are related to EMR, such as EC2, S3, and RDS, is also included.

Chapter 2, MapReduce, covers the introduction to the MapReduce paradigm of programming. It also covers the basics of the MapReduce style of programming along with the architectural data flow which happens in any MapReduce framework.

Chapter 3, Apache Hadoop, provides an introduction to Apache Hadoop among all the distributions available, as this is the most commonly used distribution on EMR. It also discusses the various components and modules of Apache Hadoop.

Chapter 4, Amazon EMR – Hadoop on Amazon Web Services, introduces the EMR service and describes its benefits. Also, a few common use cases that are solved using EMR are highlighted.

Chapter 5, Programming Hadoop on Amazon EMR, has the solution to the example problem discussed in *Chapter 2, MapReduce*. The various parts of the code will be explained using a simple problem which can be considered to be a Hello World problem in Hadoop.

Chapter 6, Executing Hadoop Jobs on an Amazon EMR Cluster, lets the user to launch a cluster on EMR, submit the wordcount job created in *Chapter 3, Apache Hadoop*, and download and view the results. There are various ways to execute jobs on Amazon EMR, and this chapter explains them with examples.

Chapter 7, Amazon EMR – Cluster Management, explains how to manage the life cycle of a cluster on an Amazon EMR. Also, the various ways available to do so are discussed separately. Planning and troubleshooting a cluster are also covered.

Chapter 8, Amazon EMR – Command-line Interface Client, provides the most useful options available with the Ruby client provided by Amazon for EMR. We will also see how to use spot instances with EMR.

Chapter 9, Hadoop Streaming and Advanced Hadoop Customizations, teaches how to use scripting languages such as Python or Ruby to create mappers and reducers instead of using Java. We will see how to launch a streaming EMR cluster and also how to add a streaming Job Step to an already running cluster.

Chapter 10, Use Case – Analyzing CloudFront Logs Using Amazon EMR, consolidates all the learning and applies them to solve a real-world use case.

What you need for this book

You will need the following software components to gain professional-level expertise with EMR:

- JDK 7 (Java 7)
- Eclipse IDE (the latest version)
- Hadoop 2.2.0
- Ruby 1.9.2
- RubyGems 1.8+
- An EMR CLI client
- Tableau Desktop
- MySQL 5.6 (the community edition)

Some of the images and screenshots used in this book are taken from the AWS website.

Who this book is for

This book is for developers and system administrators who want to learn Big Data analysis using Amazon EMR, and basic Java programming knowledge is required. You should be comfortable with using command-line tools. Experience with any scripting language such as Ruby or Python will be useful. Prior knowledge of the AWS API and CLI tools is not assumed. Also, an exposure to Hadoop and MapReduce is not required.

After reading this book, you will become familiar with the MapReduce paradigm of programming and will learn to build analytical solutions using the Hadoop framework. You will also learn to execute those solutions over Amazon EMR.

Conventions

In this book, you will find a number of styles of text that distinguish between different kinds of information. Here are some examples of these styles, and an explanation of their meaning.

Code words in text, database table names, folder names, filenames, file extensions, pathnames, dummy URLs, user input, and Twitter handles are shown as follows: "You can use the chmod command to set appropriate permissions over the .pem file."

A block of code is set as follows:

```
FileInputFormat.setInputPaths(job, args[0]);
FileOutputFormat.setOutputPath(job, new Path(args[1]));
```

When we wish to draw your attention to a particular part of a code block, the relevant lines or items are set in bold:

```
export JAVA_HOME=${JAVA_HOME}
```

Any command-line input or output is written as follows:

```
$ cd /<hadoop-2.2.0-base-path>/bin
```

New terms and **important words** are shown in bold. Words that you see on the screen, in menus or dialog boxes for example, appear in the text like this: "Click on **Browse** and select our driver class (**HitsByCountry**) from the list. Click on **OK** and then click on **Finish**."

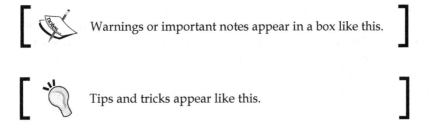

> Warnings or important notes appear in a box like this.

> Tips and tricks appear like this.

Reader feedback

Feedback from our readers is always welcome. Let us know what you think about this book—what you liked or may have disliked. Reader feedback is important for us to develop titles that you really get the most out of.

To send us general feedback, simply send an e-mail to feedback@packtpub.com, and mention the book title via the subject of your message.

If you have any feedback or have noticed any issues with respect to content, examples, and instructions in this book, you can contact the authors at emrhadoopbook@gmail.com.

Customer support

Now that you are the proud owner of a Packt book, we have a number of things to help you to get the most from your purchase.

Downloading the example code

You can download the example code files for all Packt books you have purchased from your account at http://www.packtpub.com. If you purchased this book elsewhere, you can visit http://www.packtpub.com/support and register to have the files e-mailed directly to you.

Errata

Although we have taken every care to ensure the accuracy of our content, mistakes do happen. If you find a mistake in one of our books—maybe a mistake in the text or the code—we would be grateful if you would report this to us. By doing so, you can save other readers from frustration and help us improve subsequent versions of this book. If you find any errata, please report them by visiting http://www.packtpub.com/submit-errata, selecting your book, clicking on the **errata submission form** link, and entering the details of your errata. Once your errata are verified, your submission will be accepted and the errata will be uploaded on our website, or added to any list of existing errata, under the Errata section of that title. Any existing errata can be viewed by selecting your title from http://www.packtpub.com/support.

Piracy

Piracy of copyright material on the Internet is an ongoing problem across all media. At Packt, we take the protection of our copyright and licenses very seriously. If you come across any illegal copies of our works, in any form, on the Internet, please provide us with the location address or website name immediately so that we can pursue a remedy.

Please contact us at `copyright@packtpub.com` with a link to the suspected pirated material.

We appreciate your help in protecting our authors, and our ability to bring you valuable content.

Questions

You can contact us at `questions@packtpub.com` if you are having a problem with any aspect of the book, and we will do our best to address it.

1

Amazon Web Services

Before we can start getting on with the Big Data technologies, we will first have a look at what infrastructure we will be using, which will enable us to focus more on the implementation of solutions to Big Data problems rather than spending time and resources on managing the infrastructure needed to execute those solutions. The cloud technologies have democratized access to high-scale utility computing, which was earlier available only to large companies. This is where Amazon Web Services comes to our rescue as one of the leading players in the public cloud computing landscape.

What is Amazon Web Services?

As the name suggests, **Amazon Web Services (AWS)** is a set of cloud computing services provided by Amazon that are accessible over the Internet. Since anybody can sign up and use it, AWS is classified as a public cloud computing provider.

Most of the businesses depend on applications running on a set of compute and storage resources that needs to be reliable and secure and shall scale as and when required. The latter attribute required in there, scaling, is one of the major problems with the traditional data center approach. If the business provisions too many resources expecting heavy usage of their applications, they might need to invest a lot of upfront capital (CAPEX) on their IT. Now, what if they do not receive the expected traffic? Also, if the business provisions fewer resources expecting lesser traffic and ends up with receiving more than expected traffic, they would surely have disgruntled customers and bad experience.

AWS provides scalable compute services, highly durable storage services, and low-latency database services among others to enable businesses to quickly provision the required infrastructure for the business to launch and run applications. Almost everything that you can do on a traditional data center can be achieved with AWS. AWS brings in the ability to add and remove compute resources elastically. You can start with the number of resources you expect is required, and as you go, you can scale it up to meet increasing traffic or to meet specific customer requirements. Alternatively, you may scale it down any time as required, saving money and having the flexibility to make required changes quickly. Hence, you need not invest a huge capital upfront or worry about capacity planning. Also, with AWS, you only need to pay-per-use. So, for example, if you have a business that needs more resources during a specific time of day, say for a couple of hours, with AWS, you may configure it to add resources for you and then scale down automatically as specified. In this case, you only pay for the added extra resources for those couple of hours of usage. Many businesses have leveraged AWS in this fashion to support their requirements and reduce costs.

How does AWS provide infrastructure at such low cost and at pay-per-use? The answer lies in AWS having huge number of customers spread across almost all over the world—allowing AWS to have the economies of scale, which lets AWS bring quality resources at a low operational cost to us.

Experiments and ideas that were once constrained on cost or resources are very much feasible now with AWS, resulting in increased capacity for businesses to innovate and deliver higher quality products to their customers.

Hence, AWS enables businesses around the world to focus on delivering quality experience to their customers, while AWS takes care of the heavy lifting required to launch and keep running those applications at an expected scale, securely and reliably.

Structure and Design

In this age of Internet, businesses cater to customers worldwide. Keeping that in mind, AWS has its resources physically available at multiple geographical locations spread across the world. Also, in order to recover data and applications from disasters and natural calamities, it is prudent to have resources spread across multiple geographical locations.

We have two different levels of geographical separation in AWS:

- Regions
- Availability zones

Regions

The top-level geographical separation is termed as regions on AWS. Each region is completely enclosed in a single country. The data generated and uploaded to an AWS resource resides in the region where the resource has been created.

Each region is completely independent from the other. No data/resources are replicated across regions unless the replication is explicitly performed. Any communication between resources in two different regions happens via the public Internet (unless a private network is established by the end user); hence, it's your responsibility to use proper encryption methods to secure your data.

As of now, AWS has nine operational regions across the world, with the tenth one starting soon in Beijing. The following are the available regions of AWS:

Region code	Region name
ap-northeast-1	Asia Pacific (Tokyo)
ap-southeast-1	Asia Pacific (Singapore)
ap-southeast-2	Asia Pacific (Sydney)
eu-west-1	EU (Ireland)
sa-east-1	South America (Sao Paulo)
us-east-1	US East (Northern Virginia)
us-west-1	US West (Northern California)
us-west-1	US West (Oregon)

In addition to the aforementioned regions, there are the following two regions:

- **AWS GovCloud (US)**: This is available only for the use of the US Government.
- **China (Beijing)**: At the time of this writing, this region didn't have public access and you need to request an account to create infrastructure there. It is officially available at https://www.amazonaws.cn/.

The following world map shows how AWS has its regions spread across the world:

This image has been taken from the AWS website

Availability Zones

Each region is composed of one or more availability zones. Availability zones are isolated from one another but are connected via low-latency network to provide high availability and fault tolerance within a region for AWS services. Availability zones are distinct locations present within a region. The core computing resources such as machines and storage devices are physically present in one of these availability zones. All availability zones are separated physically in order to cope up with situations, where one physical data center, for example, has a power outage or network issue or any other location-dependent issues.

Availability zones are designed to be isolated from the failures of other availability zones in the same region. Each availability zone has its own independent infrastructure. Each of them has its own independent electricity power setup and supply. The network and security setups are also detached from other availability zones, though there is low latency and inexpensive connectivity between them.

Basically, you may consider that each availability zone is a distinct physical data center. So, if there is a heating problem in one of the availability zones, other availability zones in the same region will not be hampered.

The following diagram shows the relationship between regions and availability zones:

Customers can benefit from this global infrastructure of AWS in the following ways:

- Achieve low latency for application requests by serving from locations nearer to the origin of the request. So, if you have your customers in Australia, you would want to serve requests from the Sydney region.

- Comply with legal requirements. Keeping data within a region helps some of the customers to comply with requirements of various countries where sending user's data out of the country isn't allowed.

- Build fault tolerance and high availability applications, which can tolerate failures in one data center.

When you launch a machine on AWS, you will be doing so in a selected region; further, you can select one of the availability zones in which you want your machine to be launched. You may distribute your instances (or machines) across multiple availability zones and have your application serve requests from a machine in another availability zone when the machine fails in one of the availability zones.

You may also use another service AWS provide, namely Elastic IP addresses, to mask the failure of a machine in one availability zone by rapidly remapping the address to a machine in another availability zone where other machine is working fine.

This architecture enables AWS to have a very high level of fault tolerance and, hence, provides a highly available infrastructure for businesses to run their applications on.

Services provided by AWS

AWS provides a wide variety of global services catering to large enterprises as well as smart start-ups. As of today, AWS provides a growing set of over 60 services across various sectors of a cloud infrastructure. All of the services provided by AWS can be accessed via the AWS management console (a web portal) or programmatically via API (or web services). We will learn about the most popular ones and which are most used across industries.

AWS categorizes its services into the following major groups:

- Compute
- Storage
- Database
- Network and CDN
- Analytics
- Application services
- Deployment and management

Let's now discuss all the groups and list down the services available in each one of them.

Compute

The compute group of services includes the most basic service provided by AWS: Amazon EC2, which is like a virtual compute machine. AWS provides a wide range of virtual machine types; in AWS lingo, they are called instances.

Amazon EC2

EC2 stands for **Elastic Compute Cloud**. The key word is *elastic*. EC2 is a web service that provides resizable compute capacity in the AWS Cloud. Basically, using this service, you can provision instances of varied capacity on a cloud. You can launch instances within minutes and you can terminate them when work is done. You can decide on the computing capacity of your instance, that is, number of CPU cores or amount of memory, among others from a pool of machine types offered by AWS.

You only pay for usage of instances by number of hours. It may be noted here that if you run an instance for one hour and few minutes, it will be billed as 2 hours. Each partial instance hour consumed is billed as full hour. We will learn about EC2 in more detail in the next section.

Auto Scaling

Auto scaling is one of the popular services AWS has built and offers to customers to handle spikes in application loads by adding or removing infrastructure capacity. Auto scaling allows you to define conditions; when these conditions are met, AWS would automatically scale your compute capacity up or down. This service is well suited for applications that have time dependency on its usage or predictable spikes in the usage.

Auto scaling also helps in the scenario where you want your application infrastructure to have a fixed number of machines always available to it. You can configure this service to automatically check the health of each of the machines and add capacity as and when required if there are any issues with existing machines. This helps you to ensure that your application receives the compute capacity it requires.

Moreover, this service doesn't have additional pricing, only EC2 capacity being used is billed.

Elastic Load Balancing

Elastic Load Balancing (ELB) is the load balancing service provided by AWS. ELB automatically distributes the incoming application's traffic among multiple EC2 instances. This service helps in achieving high availability for applications by load balancing traffic across multiple instances in different availability zones for fault tolerance.

ELB has the capability to automatically scale its capacity to handle requests to match the demands of the application's traffic. It also offers integration with auto scaling, wherein you may configure it to also scale the backend capacity to cater to the varying traffic levels without manual intervention.

Amazon Workspaces

The Amazon Workspaces service provides cloud-based desktops for on-demand usage by businesses. It is a fully managed desktop computing service in the cloud. It allows you to access your documents and applications from anywhere and from devices of your choice. You can choose the hardware and software as per your requirement. It allows you to choose from packages providing different amounts of CPU, memory, and storage.

Amazon Workspaces also have the facility to securely integrate with your corporate Active Directory.

Storage

Storage is another group of essential services. AWS provides low-cost data storage services having high durability and availability. AWS offers storage choices for backup, archiving, and disaster recovery, as well as block, file, and object storage. As is the nature of most of the services on AWS, for storage too, you pay as you go.

Amazon S3

S3 stands for **Simple Storage Service**. S3 provides a simple web service interface with fully redundant data storage infrastructure to store and retrieve any amount of data at any time and from anywhere on the Web. Amazon uses S3 to run its own global network of websites.

As AWS states:

> *Amazon S3 is cloud storage for the Internet.*

Amazon S3 can be used as a storage medium for various purposes. We will read about it in more detail in the next section.

Amazon EBS

EBS stands for **Elastic Block Store**. It is one of the most used service of AWS. It provides block-level storage volumes to be used with EC2 instances. While the instance storage data cannot be persisted after the instance has been terminated, using EBS volumes you can persist your data independently from the life cycle of an instance to which the volumes are attached to. EBS is sometimes also termed as off-instance storage.

EBS provides consistent and low-latency performance. Its reliability comes from the fact that each EBS volume is automatically replicated within its availability zone to protect you from hardware failures. It also provides the ability to copy snapshots of volumes across AWS regions, which enables you to migrate data and plan for disaster recovery.

Amazon Glacier

Amazon Glacier is an extremely low-cost storage service targeted at data archival and backup. Amazon Glacier is optimized for infrequent access of data. You can reliably store your data that you do not want to read frequently with a cost as low as $0.01 per GB per month.

AWS commits to provide average annual durability of 99.999999999 percent for an archive. This is achieved by redundantly storing data in multiple locations and on multiple devices within one location. Glacier automatically performs regular data integrity checks and has automatic self-healing capability.

AWS Storage Gateway

AWS Storage Gateway is a service that enables secure and seamless connection between on-premise software appliance with AWS's storage infrastructure. It provides low-latency reads by maintaining an on-premise cache of frequently accessed data while all the data is stored securely on Amazon S3 or Glacier.

In case you need low-latency access to your entire dataset, you can configure this service to store data locally and asynchronously back up point-in-time snapshots of this data to S3.

AWS Import/Export

The **AWS Import/Export** service accelerates moving large amounts of data into and out of AWS infrastructure using portable storage devices for transport. Data transfer via Internet might not always be the feasible way to move data to and from AWS's storage services.

Using this service, you can import data into Amazon S3, Glacier, or EBS. It is also helpful in disaster recovery scenarios where in you might need to quickly retrieve a large amount of data backup stored in S3 or Glacier; using this service, your data can be transferred to a portable storage device and delivered to your site.

Databases

AWS provides fully managed relational and NoSQL database services. It also has one fully managed in-memory caching as a service and a fully managed data-warehouse service. You can also use Amazon EC2 and EBS to host any database of your choice.

Amazon RDS

RDS stands for **Relational Database Service**. With database systems, setup, backup, and upgrading are the tasks, which are tedious and at the same time critical. RDS aims to free you of these responsibilities and lets you focus on your application. RDS supports all the major databases, namely, MySQL, Oracle, SQL Server, and PostgreSQL. It also provides the capability to resize the instances holding these databases as per the load. Similarly, it provides a facility to add more storage as and when required.

Amazon RDS makes it just a matter of few clicks to use replication to enhance availability and reliability for production workloads. Using its **Multi-AZ deployment** option, you can run very critical applications with high availability and in-built automated failover. It synchronously replicates data to a secondary database. On failure of the primary database, Amazon RDS automatically starts fetching data for further requests from the replicated secondary database.

Amazon DynamoDB

Amazon DynamoDB is a fully managed NoSQL database service mainly aimed at applications requiring single-digit millisecond latency. There is no limit to the amount of data you can store in DynamoDB. It uses an SSD-storage, which helps in providing very high performance.

DynamoDB is a schemaless database. Tables do not need to have fixed schemas. Each record may have a different number of columns. Unlike many other nonrelational databases, DynamoDB ensures strong read consistency, making sure that you always read the latest value.

DynamoDB also integrates with **Amazon Elastic MapReduce (Amazon EMR)**. With DynamoDB, it is easy for customers to use Amazon EMR to analyze datasets stored in DynamoDB and archive the results in **Amazon S3**.

Amazon Redshift

Amazon Redshift is basically a modern data warehouse system. It is an enterprise-class relational query and management system. It is PostgreSQL compliant, which means you may use most of the SQL commands to query tables in Redshift.

Amazon Redshift achieves efficient storage and great query performance through a combination of various techniques. These include massively parallel processing infrastructures, columnar data storage, and very efficient targeted data compressions encoding schemes as per the column data type. It has the capability of automated backups and fast restores. There are in-built commands to import data directly from S3, DynamoDB, or your on-premise servers to Redshift.

You can configure Redshift to use SSL to secure data transmission. You can also set it up to encrypt data at rest, for which Redshift uses hardware-accelerated AES-256 encryption.

As we will see in *Chapter 10, Use Case – Analyzing CloudFront Logs Using Amazon EMR*, Redshift can be used as the data store to efficiently analyze all your data using existing business intelligence tools such as Tableau or Jaspersoft. Many of these existing business intelligence tools have in-built capabilities or plugins to work with Redshift.

Amazon ElastiCache

Amazon ElastiCache is basically an in-memory cache cluster service in cloud. It makes life easier for developers by loading off most of the operational tasks. Using this service, your applications can fetch data from fast in-memory caches for some frequently needed information or for some counters kind of data.

Amazon ElastiCache supports two most commonly used open source in-memory caching engines:

* Memcached
* Redis

As with other AWS services, Amazon ElastiCache is also fully managed, which means it automatically detects and replaces failed nodes.

Networking and CDN

Networking and CDN services include the networking services that let you create logically isolated networks in cloud, the setup of a private network connection to the AWS cloud, and an easy-to-use DNS service. AWS also has one content delivery network service that lets you deliver content to your users with higher speeds.

Amazon VPC

VPC stands for **Virtual Private Cloud**. As the name suggests, AWS allows you to set up an isolated section of AWS cloud, which is private. You can launch resources to be available only inside that private network. It allows you to create subnets and then create resources within those subnets. With EC2 instances without VPC, one internal and one external IP addresses are always assigned; but with VPC, you have control over the IP of your resource; you may choose to only keep an internal IP for a machine. In effect, that machine will only be known by other machines on that subnet; hence, providing a greater level of control over security of your cloud infrastructure.

You can further control the security of your cloud infrastructure by using features such as security groups and network access control lists. You can configure inbound and outbound filtering at instance level as well as at subnet level.

You can connect your entire VPC to your on-premise data center.

Amazon Route 53

Amazon Route 53 is simply a **Domain Name System (DNS)** service that translates names to IP addresses and provides low-latency responses to DNS queries by using its global network of DNS servers.

Amazon CloudFront

Amazon CloudFront is a CDN service provided by AWS. Amazon CloudFront has a network of delivery centers called as **edge locations** all around the world. Static contents are cached on the edge locations closer to the requests for those contents, effecting into lowered latency for further downloads of those contents. Requests for your content are automatically routed to the nearest edge location, so content is delivered with the best possible performance.

AWS Direct Connect

If you do not trust Internet to connect to AWS services, you may use this service. Using **AWS Direct Connect**, a private connectivity can be established between your data center and AWS. You may also want to use this service to reduce your network costs and have more consistent network performance.

Analytics

Analytics is the group of services, which host Amazon EMR among others. These are a set of services that help you to process and analyze huge volumes of data.

Amazon EMR

The Amazon EMR service lets you process any amount of data by launching a cluster of required number of instances, and this cluster will have one of the analytics engines predeployed. EMR mainly provides Hadoop and related tools such as Pig, Hive, and HBase. People who have spent hours in deploying a Hadoop cluster will understand the importance of EMR. Within minutes, you can launch a Hadoop cluster having hundreds of instances. Also, you can resize your cluster on the go with a few simple commands. We will be learning more about EMR throughout this book.

Amazon Kinesis

Amazon Kinesis is a service for real-time streaming data collection and processing. It can collect and process hundreds of terabytes of data per hour from hundreds of thousands of sources, as claimed by AWS. It allows you to write applications to process data in real time from sources such as log streams, clickstreams, and many more. You can build real-time dashboards showing current trends, recent changes/improvements, failures, and errors.

AWS Data Pipeline

AWS Data Pipeline is basically a service to automate a data pipeline. That is, using this, you can reliably move data between various AWS resources at scheduled times and on meeting some preconditions. For instance, you receive daily logs in your S3 buckets and you need to process them using EMR and move the output to a Redshift table. All of this can be automated using AWS Data Pipeline, and you will get processed data moved to Redshift on daily basis ready to be queried by your BI tool.

Application services

Application services include services, which you can use with applications. These include search functionality, queuing service, push notifications, and e-mail delivery among others.

Amazon CloudSearch (Beta)

Amazon CloudSearch is a search service that allows you to easily integrate fast and highly scalable search functionality into your applications. It now supports 34 languages. It also supports popular search features such as highlighting, autocomplete, and geospatial search.

Amazon SQS

SQS stands for **Simple Queue Service**. It provides a hosted queue to store messages as they are transferred between computers. It ensures that no messages are lost, as all messages are stored redundantly across multiple servers and data centers.

Amazon SNS

SNS stands for **Simple Notification Service**. It is basically a push messaging service. It allows you to push messages to mobile devices or distributed services. You can anytime seamlessly scale from a few messages a day to thousands of messages per hour.

Amazon SES

SES stands for **Simple Email Service**. It is basically an e-mail service for the cloud. You can use it for sending bulk and transactional e-mails. It provides real-time access to sending statistics and also provides alerts on delivery failures.

Amazon AppStream

Amazon AppStream is a service that helps you to stream heavy applications such as games or videos to your customers.

Amazon Elastic Transcoder

Amazon Elastic Transcoder is a service that lets you transcode media. It is a fully managed service that makes it easy to convert media files in the cloud with scalability and at a low cost.

Amazon SWF

SWF stands for **Simple Workflow Service**. It is a task coordination and state management service for various applications running on AWS.

Deployment and Management

Deployment and Management groups have services which AWS provides you to help with the deployment and management of your applications on AWS cloud infrastructure. This also includes services to monitor your applications and keep track of your AWS API activities.

AWS Identity and Access Management

The AWS **Identity and Access Management (IAM)** service enables you to create fine-grained control access to AWS services and resources for your users.

Amazon CloudWatch

Amazon CloudWatch is a web service that provides monitoring for various AWS cloud resources. It collects metrics specific to the resource. It also allows you to programmatically access your monitoring data and build graphs or set alarms to help you better manage your infrastructure. Basic monitoring metrics (at 5-minute frequency) for Amazon EC2 instances are free of charge. It will cost you if you opt for detailed monitoring. For pricing, you can refer to `http://aws.amazon.com/cloudwatch/pricing/`.

AWS Elastic Beanstalk

AWS Elastic Beanstalk is a service that helps you to easily deploy web applications and services built on popular programming languages such as Java, .NET, PHP, Node.js, Python, and Ruby. There is no additional charge for this service; you only pay for the underlying AWS infrastructure that you create for your application.

AWS CloudFormation

AWS CloudFormation is a service that provides you with an easy way to create a set of related AWS resources and provision them in an orderly and predictable fashion. This service makes it easier to replicate a working cloud infrastructure. There are various templates provided by AWS; you may use any one of them as it is or you can create your own.

AWS OpsWorks

AWS OpsWorks is a service built for DevOps. It is an application management service that makes it easy to manage an entire application stack from load balancers to databases.

AWS CloudHSM

The **AWS CloudHSM** service allows you to use dedicated **Hardware Security Module (HSM)** appliances within the AWS Cloud. You may need to meet some corporate, contractual, or regulatory compliance requirements for data security, which you can achieve by using CloudHSM.

AWS CloudTrail

AWS CloudTrail is simply a service that logs API requests to AWS from your account. It logs API requests to AWS from all the available sources such as AWS Management Console, various AWS SDKs, and command-line tools.

AWS keeps on adding useful and innovative products to its repository of already vast set of services. AWS is clearly the leader among the cloud infrastructure providers.

AWS Pricing

Amazon provides a Free Tier across AWS products and services in order to help you get started and gain hands-on experience before you can build your solutions on top. Using a Free Tier, you can test your applications and gain the confidence required before a full-fledged use.

The following table lists some of the common services and what you can get in the Free Tier for them:

Service	Free Tier limit
Amazon EC2	750 hours per month of the Linux, RHEL, or SLES `t2.micro` instance usage
	750 hours per month of the Windows `t2.micro` instance usage
Amazon S3	5 GB of standard storage, 20,000 `Get` requests, and 2,000 `Put` requests
Amazon EBS	30 GB of Amazon EBS: any combination of general purpose (SSD) or magnetic
	2,000,000 I/Os (with EBS magnetic) and 1 GB of snapshot storage
Amazon RDS	750 hours per month of micro DB instance usage
	20 GB of DB storage, 20 GB for backups, and 10,000,000 I/Os

The Free Tier is available only for the first 12 months from the sign up for new customers. When your 12 months expire or if your usage exceeds the Free Tier limits, you will need to pay standard rates, which AWS calls pay-as-you-go service rates. You can refer to each service's page for pricing details. For example, in order to get the pricing detail for EC2, you may refer to `http://aws.amazon.com/ec2/pricing/`.

> You should keep a tab on your usage and use any service after you know that the pricing and your expected usage matches your budget. In order to track your AWS usage, sign in to the AWS management console and open the Billing and Cost Management console at `https://console.aws.amazon.com/billing/home#/`.

Creating an account on AWS

Signing up for AWS is very simple and straightforward. The following is a step-by-step guide for you to create an account on AWS and launch the AWS management console.

Step 1 – Creating an Amazon.com account

Go to `http://aws.amazon.com` and click on **Sign Up**.

This will take you to a page saying **Sign In or Create an AWS Account**. If you already have an `Amazon.com` account, you can use this to start using AWS; or you can create a new account by selecting **I am a new user** and clicking on **Sign in using our secure server**:

Further, you will need to key in the basic login information such as password, contact information, and other account details and create an `Amazon.com` account and continue.

Step 2 – Providing a payment method

You will need to provide your payment information to AWS. You will not be charged up front, but will be charged for the AWS resources you will use.

Step 3 – Identity verification by telephone

In order to complete the sign-up process, AWS needs to verify your identity. After you provide a phone number where you can be reached, you will receive a call immediately from an automated system and will be prompted to enter the PIN number over the phone. Only when this done, you will be able to proceed further.

Step 4 – Selecting the AWS support plan

There are various levels of support available from AWS, and you can choose from the following four packages:

- **Basic**
- **Developer**
- **Business**
- **Enterprise**

That's all. You have your AWS account created and you are ready-to-use AWS.

Launching the AWS management console

Go to `https://console.aws.amazon.com` and sign in using the account you just created. This will take you to a screen displaying a list of AWS services. After you start using AWS more and more, you can configure any particular service page to be your landing page:

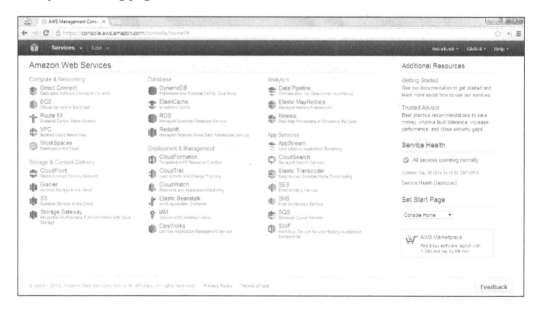

The resources are listed on per region basis. That is, first a region needs to be selected and then only you can view the resources tied to that region. AWS resources are global, tied to a region, or tied to an availability zone.

Getting started with Amazon EC2

EC2 is the most basic web service provided by AWS. It allows you to launch instances of various capacities. You can get complete control over the lifetime of this instance, and you also have the root access.

How to start a machine on AWS?

After you sign in to your AWS console, you can start a machine in a few steps. Go to the EC2-specific console view from your AWS console. Select the region in which you want to launch your instance. This can be selected from the top-right corner of the page.

Click on **Launch Instance**. Let's walk through the simple steps you need to follow after this.

Step 1 – Choosing an Amazon Machine Image

Amazon Machine Image (**AMI**) is a set of predefined software configuration and applications. It is basically a template that contains the details about operating system, application server, and initial set of applications required to launch your instance. There are a set of standard AMIs provided by AWS, there are AMIs contributed by the user community, and also there are AMIs available in the AWS marketplace. You can select an AMI from among them. If you are confused, select one of the AMIs from the **Quick Start** section.

Step 2 – Choosing an instance type

AWS EC2 provides various instance types optimized to fit different use cases. A virtual machine launched on AWS is called as an instance. They have varying combinations of CPU, memory, storage, and networking capacity giving you the liberty to decide on the right set of computing resources for your applications.

Choose the instance type that fits your needs and budget. If you are just trying out things, you may go for **t1.micro**, which is available under Free Tier. We will discuss about instance types in more detail in our next section.

At this stage, you may skip other steps and go ahead and launch your instance. However, that is not recommended, as your machine would be open to the world, that is, it will be publicly accessible. AWS provides with a feature for creating security groups, wherein you can create inbound and outbound rules restricting unwanted traffic and only allowing some trusted IPs to connect to your instance.

Step 3 – Configuring instance details

In this step, you may instruct AWS to launch multiple instances of the same type and with the same AMI. You may also choose to request for spot instance. Additionally, you can add the following configurations to your instance:

- The network your instance will belong to. Here, you choose the VPC of which you want your instance to be a part of. After selecting a VPC, if you want, you may also let AWS automatically assign a public IP address to your instance. This IP will only be associated with your instance until it is stopped or terminated.

- The availability zone your instance will belong to. This can be set if you do not select a VPC and go with the default network, that is, **EC2-Classic**.

- The IAM role, if any, you want to assign to your instance.

- The instance behavior when an OS-level shut down is performed. It is recommended to keep this configuration to **Stop**. Instances can be either terminated or stopped.

You can also enable the protection from accidental termination of the instance. Once this is enabled, you cannot terminate it from the AWS management console or using AWS APIs until you disable this. You can also enable CloudWatch detailed monitoring for this instance.

Step 4 – Adding storage

Every instance type comes with a definite instance storage. You can attach more instance storage volumes or may decide to add EBS volumes to your instance. EBS volumes can also be attached later after launching the instance. You can also edit the configurations of the root volume of your instance.

Step 5 – Tagging your instance

For better book-keeping purposes, it is always good to give a name to your instance, for example, MyApplicationWebserverBox. You can also create custom tags suiting your needs.

Step 6 – Configuring a security group

You can create a new security group for your instance or you can use an already defined security group. For example, if you already have a few web servers and you are just adding another instance to that group of servers, you wouldn't want to create a separate security group for that, rather you can reuse the existing security group that was created for those web servers.

While creating a new security group, you will see that one entry is prefilled to enable remote login to that machine via SSH from anywhere. If you want, you can constrain that rule to allow SSH traffic only via fixed IPs or IP ranges. Similarly, you can add rules for other protocols. If you have a web server running and you want to open the HTTP traffic for the world or if you have a MySQL database running on this machine, you would want to select **MySQL** from the type while adding a new rule and set the **Source** setting to your machines from where you would want your MySQL to be accessible.

You can now review your configurations and settings and launch your instance. Just one small thing before your instance is launched: you need to specify the key pair in order to access this instance remotely. You can choose an existing key pair or can create a new key pair. You must download the private key file (*.pem) and keep it securely. You would use this to SSH into this instance.

 It is very important to note that if this private key file is lost, there is no way to log in to the instance after it is launched. As AWS doesn't store the private key at its end, keep it securely.

That's all. Click on **Launch Instances**. Your instance should be up and running within minutes.

If you go back to the EC2 dashboard of your AWS management console, you will see that your instance is added to the number of running instances. Your EC2 dashboard view will look as follows:

Resources	
You are using the following Amazon EC2 resources in the US West (Oregon) region:	
1 Running Instances	0 Elastic IPs
0 Volumes	0 Snapshots
0 Key Pairs	0 Load Balancers
0 Placement Groups	1 Security Group

Communicating with the launched instance

After launching your instance, when you click on the link saying **n Running Instances**, where **n** is the number of instances running, you will be taken to a page having all the running instances listed. There, you should select the instance you had launched; you can identify it from the name you had given while launching the instance. Now, in the bottom pane, you can see the **Public DNS** and **Public IP** values listed for the selected instance (let's assume that you had configured your instance to be provided a public IP while launching). You will use either of these values to SSH into your instance.

Let's assume the following before moving ahead:

- Public IP of your machine is `51:215:203:111` (this is some random IP just for the sake of explanation)

- Public DNS of your machine is `ec2-51-215-203-111.ap-southeast-1.compute.amazonaws.com` (your instance's public DNS will look like this given the above IP and that your instance was launched in the Singapore region)

- Private key file path in the machine from where you want to connect to newly launched instance is `/home/awesomeuser/secretkeys/my-private-key.pem`

Now that you have all the information about your instance, connecting to the instance is only a matter of one SSH command. You should ensure that you have an SSH client installed on the machine from where you will connect to your AWS instance. For Linux-based machines, a command-line SSH client is readily available.

As the private key pair is very critical from security point of view, it is important to set the appropriate access control to this file so that it isn't publicly viewable. You can use the `chmod` command to set appropriate permissions over the `.pem` file:

```
chmod 400 my-key-pair.pem
```

You can connect to your instance by executing the following command from the command line:

```
$ssh -i /home/awesomeuser/secretkeys/my-private-key.pem ec2-user@ec2-51-215-203-111.ap-southeast-1.compute.amazonaws.com
```

Alternatively, you can also connect using the public IP:

```
$ssh -i  /home/awesomeuser/secretkeys/my-private-key.pem ec2-user@51:215:203:111
```

You may note that the username to log in is `ec2-user`. You can assume root access by simply switching user by the following command, you won't be prompted for a password:

```
$ sudo su
```

> For Windows machines, you can also use a simple connectivity tool such as Putty to SSH to your instance.

EC2 instance types

EC2 has several predefined capacity packages that you can choose to launch an instance with. Instance types are defined and categorized based on the following parameters:

- CPU
- Memory
- Storage
- Network Capacity

Each instance type in turn includes multiple instance sizes for you to choose from. Primarily, there are three most commonly used instance types:

- General purpose: M3
- Memory optimized: R3
- Compute optimized : C3

General purpose

The general purpose set of instances consists of M3 instance types. These types of instances have a balance of compute, memory, and network resources. They have SSD-based instance storage.

M3 instance sizes

The following table lists the instances sized for M3 instance types:

Instance size	vCPU	Memory (GB)	Storage (GB)
m3.medium	1	3.75	1 * 4
m3.large	2	7.5	1 * 32
m3.xlarge	4	15	2 * 40
m3.2xlarge	8	30	2 * 80

As you can see, with every increasing instance size, CPU and memory gets doubled.

Memory optimized

This set of instances consists of R3 instance types. These types of instances are best fit for memory-intensive applications. R3 instances have the lowest cost per GB of RAM among all EC2 instance types.

These types of instances are suitable for in-memory analytics, distributed-memory-based caching engines, and many other similar memory-intensive applications.

R3 instance sizes

The following table lists the instances sized for R3 instance types:

Instance size	vCPU	Memory (GB)	Storage (GB)
r3.large	2	15	1 * 32
r3.2large	4	30.5	1 * 80
r3.4xlarge	8	61	1 * 160
r3.4xlarge	16	122	1 * 320
r3.8xlarge	32	244	2 * 320

Compute optimized

This set of instances consists of C3 instance types. These types of instances are best fit for compute-intensive applications. C3 instances have the highest performing processors and the lowest price / compute performance available in EC2 currently.

These types of instances are suitable for high performance applications such as on-demand batch-processing, video encoding, high-end gaming, and many other similar compute-intensive applications.

C3 instance sizes

The following table lists the instances sized for C3 instance types:

Instance size	vCPU	Memory (GB)	Storage (GB)
c3.large	2	3.75	2 * 16
c3.2large	4	7.5	2 * 40
c3.4xlarge	8	15	2 * 80
c3.4xlarge	16	30	2 * 160
c3. 8xlarge	32	60	2 * 320

There are other instance types such as GPU, which are mainly used for game streaming, and storage optimized instance types, which are used to create large clusters of NoSQL databases and house various data warehousing engines. Micro instance types are also available, which are the low-end instances.

Getting started with Amazon S3

S3 is a service aimed at making developers and businesses free from worrying about having enough storage available. It is a very robust and reliable service that enables you to store any amount of data and ensures that your data will be available when you need it.

Creating a S3 bucket

Creating a S3 bucket is just a matter of a few clicks and setting a few parameters such as the name of the bucket. Let's have a walk-through of the simple steps required to create a S3 bucket from the AWS management console:

1. Go to the S3 dashboard and click on **Create Bucket**.

2. Enter a bucket name of your choice and select the AWS region in which you want to create your bucket.

3. That's all, just click on **Create** and you are done.

Bucket naming

The bucket name you choose should be unique among all existing bucket names in Amazon S3. Because bucket names form a part of the URL to access its objects via HTTP, it is required to follow DNS naming conventions.

The DNS naming conventions include the following rules:

- It must be at least three and no more than 63 characters long.

- It must be a series of one or more labels. Adjacent labels are separated by a single period (.).

- It can contain lowercase letters, numbers, and hyphens.

- Each individual label within a name must start and end with a lowercase letter or a number.

- It must not be formatted as an IP address.

Some examples of valid and invalid bucket names are listed in the following table:

Invalid bucket name	Valid bucket name
TheAwesomeBucket	the.awesome.bucket
.theawesomebucket	theawesomebucket
the..awesomebucket	the.awesomebucket

Now, you can easily upload your files in this bucket by clicking on the bucket name and then clicking on **Upload**. You can also create folders inside the bucket.

 Apart from accessing S3 from the AWS management console, there are many independently created S3 browsers available for various operating systems. For Windows, there is **CloudBerry** and there is **Bucket Explorer** for Linux. Also, there are nice plugins available for Chrome and Firefox.

S3cmd

S3cmd is a free command-line tool to upload, retrieve, and manage data on Amazon S3. It boasts some of the advanced features such as multipart uploads, encryption, incremental backup, and S3 sync among others. You can use S3cmd to automate your S3-related tasks.

You may download the latest version of S3cmd from http://s3tools.org and check for instructions on the website regarding installing it. This is a separate open source tool that is not developed by Amazon.

In order to use S3cmd, you will need to first configure your S3 credentials. To configure credentials, you need to execute the following command:

```
s3cmd --configure
```

You will be prompted for two keys: **Access Key** and **Secret Key**. You can get these keys from the IAM dashboard of your AWS management console. You may leave default values for other configurations.

Now, by using very intuitive commands, you may access and manage your S3 buckets. These commands are mentioned in the following table:

Task	Command
List all the buckets	`s3cmd ls`
Create a bucket	`s3cmd mb s3://my.awesome.unique.bucket`
List the contents of a bucket	`s3cmd ls s3://my.awesome.unique.bucket`
Upload a file into a bucket	`s3cmd put /myfilepath/myfilename.abc s3://my.awesome.unique.bucket`
Download a file	`S3cmd get s3://my.awesome.unique.bucket/ myfilename.abc /myfilepath/`

Summary

We learned about the world of cloud computing infrastructure and got a quick introduction to AWS. We created an AWS account and discussed how to launch a machine and set up storage on S3.

In the next chapter, we will dive into the world of distributed paradigm of programming called MapReduce. The following chapters will help you understand how AWS has made it easier for businesses and developers to build and operate Big Data applications.

2
MapReduce

We will get into the *what and how* of MapReduce in a bit, but first let's say you have a simple counting problem at hand. Say, you need to count a number of hits to your website per country or per city. The only hurdle you have in solving this is the sheer amount of input data you have in order to solve this problem. That is, your website is quite popular and you have huge amounts of access logs generated per day. Also, you need to create a system in place which would send a report on a daily basis to the top management showing the number of total views per country.

Had it been a few hundred MBs of access logs or even a few GBs, you could easily create a standalone application that would crunch these data and count the views per country in a few hours. But what to do when the input data is in hundreds of GBs?

The best way to handle this will be to create a processing system that can work on parts of the input data in parallel and ultimately combine all the results. This system has to have a distributed algorithm, that is, the algorithm can be executed independently on multiple machines simultaneously on different parts of the input and it should be able to combine the results from all of those independent executions.

Using MapReduce is certainly one of the best ways available to achieve that. It is a programming model with a distributed algorithm that can be executed in parallel on a cluster.

Now, let's see how we can count the views per country, crunching large amount of access logs. While MapReduce as a framework entails many more attributes, it boils down to breaking the solution for the problem at hand into two functions:

- The map function
- The reduce function

Now, before we get into creating these two functions for our counting problem, let's clear up our input format. For simplicity, let's assume that each line in the access log may look as follows:

```
Time, Requesting-IP-Address(remote host)
```

Many other details such as the request line from client, the status code returned by server, the referrer, the user-agent identifying the browser, or application used to request the webpage, among others, are generally present in access logs. These data points can be used to add many other dimensions to the report you are going to generate for your top management. For example, they may want to know how many requests they are getting from mobile devices and whether they need to focus on improving/building/customizing their website for a particular mobile operating system.

Getting back to our counting problem, let's say we have the following lines of input:

```
T1, IP1
T2, IP2
T3, IP3
T4, IP4
T5, IP5
T6, IP1
T7, IP3
T8, IP6
T9, IP7
```

This input just signifies that we going to ignore the other details we have in our access logs and only be concerned about the IP address of the remote host requesting the web page. Using the IP address, we can find out the country from where the request has originated.

The map function

Let's design the map function now. A map function takes in a `<key,value>` pair as input and emits one or more `<key,value>` pairs. This function operates on the input value in isolation, that is, it has nothing to do with any other input values, which signifies that a map function is stateless. This is desired, as now map functions can be executed against many input data in parallel.

In our case, the map function can take one line in the access log as input value (key can be either null or an autoincrement integer), find the country to which the requesting IP belongs, and emit the output as `<Country,1>`. So for our set of input lines to map function, we will have the following lines emitted as output:

Input access log	Map output `<Key, Value>`
`T1, IP1`	`<Country1, 1>`
`T2, IP2`	`<Country2, 1>`
`T3, IP3`	`<Country3, 1>`
`T4, IP4`	`<Country1, 1>`
`T5, IP5`	`<Country3, 1>`
`T6, IP1`	`<Country1, 1>`
`T7, IP3`	`<Country3, 1>`
`T8, IP6`	`<Country2, 1>`
`T9, IP7`	`<Country1, 1>`

The reduce function

Before the reduce function comes into the picture, the MapReduce framework groups all the map output as per the key and lines up the input for the reducer. It is again formed as a key-value pair wherein the key is the same as the output of the map function, but the value is now the list of values of all those map outputs having the same key. All the preceding map outputs now get grouped as follows:

```
<Country1, [1,1,1,1]>
<Country2, [1,1]>
<Country3, [1,1,1]>
```

Each of these above aggregated key-value pairs will be fed to the reduce function. A reduce function expects a key and a list of values as input. Now, we have a super simple task of addition in the reduce function. This function just needs to add up the number of elements in the list of values it receives and emit the output key-value pair in the form of `<Country, Number-of-occurrences>`. Even reduce functions are stateless as they are isolated from the execution of other reduce functions. So, many reduce functions can run in parallel, working on a subset of map outputs.

Getting back to our problem, the output you now have after reduce functions are executed will look as follows:

```
<Country1, 4
<Country2, 2>
<Country3, 3>
```

That's all. You have your report ready for your higher management.

That's very easy, isn't it? MapReduce is very intuitive for problems of counting and summation.

Divide and conquer

If you look closely, the approach we took in the form of MapReduce is nothing but the age-old technique of **divide and conquer**. Our main problem was size of data; now with this paradigm of MapReduce, we can work on this data in parallel and get the desired results in the required timeframe. If we can break down the logical steps involved, it will be as follows:

1. *Divide* the input dataset into many chunks.
2. Execute our map function on them in parallel.
3. Start *conquering* and group the map outputs as per their key.
4. Execute our reduce function on them in parallel. *Conquered*!

Generally, the MapReduce framework will do most of the tasks for you and you will only need to worry about designing map and reduce functions and think in terms of key-value pairs as part of your solution. Tasks such as dividing the input data and grouping the map outputs are done by the framework itself. Sure, you have the option to control and customize these actions as per your needs.

What is MapReduce?

MapReduce is a style of programming model getting popular with the emergence of easily accessible distributed cloud computing. It is a programming paradigm that allows massively parallel execution and brings in the scalability required for processing huge amounts of data within desired time frames.

As for the definition, here is a quote from an abstract of the initial paper on MapReduce from Google; it says:

> *"MapReduce is a programming model and an associated implementation for processing and generating large data sets. Users specify a map function that processes a key/value pair to generate a set of intermediate key/value pairs, and a reduce function that merges all intermediate values associated with the same intermediate key.*
>
> *Programs written in this functional style are automatically parallelized and executed on a large cluster of commodity machines."*

The abstract also states that the runtime system, which will be a part of the MapReduce framework, will take care of the input data partitioning, scheduling the program's execution across multiple systems, handling failures, and managing the required inter-machine communication.

The map and reduce function in itself aren't the only driving force of the MapReduce framework; it is the scalable nature it brings to the applications that makes this framework useful in processing large datasets. This framework has been built with assumptions that machines running these systems will fail. Hence, right from the onset, it is designed to be fault tolerant.

Although this framework can be used to process even small amounts of data, its benefit can really be seen only when multiprocess, multimachine implementation is used to process large amounts of data, wherein the network communication optimizations and fault tolerance of the MapReduce framework come into play.

The map reduce function models

We have already seen in the implementation of our initial problem how a map function and reduce function is expected to behave. Now, let's see the systematic model of map and reduce functions and their expected definitions along with their limitations and possibilities.

The map function model

Each map function accepts a key-value pair as input and emits a list of key-value pairs:

Map(key-input,value-input) → List(key-map-output, value-map-output)

Two small points regarding input/output of a map function are as follows:

- In some systems, the input might just be a single value rather than a key-value pair. In these cases, the map function might be considered to have a null or empty key.

  The function will look as follows:

  Map(input-value) → List(key, value)

- The list emitted by a map function may be empty, have a single key-value pair, or have multiple key-value pairs depending on the input and the function's corresponding logic.

The reduce function model

Each reduce function accepts a key and a list of values as input and emits a list of key-value pairs. This behavior is a bit different from the traditional functional programming using map and reduce, wherein one single value is returned after the reduction:

Reduce(key-map-output, List(value-map-output)) → *List(key-output, value-output)*

Similar to the map function, the following points are correct for the reduce output:

- In some systems, the output might just be a list of single values rather than a list of key-value pairs.

  The function will look as follows:

  Reduce(key, List(value)) → *List(value)*

- The list emitted by a reduce function may be empty, have a single key-value pair, or have multiple key-value pairs depending on the map output and the function's logic.

One key take away from the above descriptions of map and reduce models is that the initial map input and reduce output can be decided by the map and reduce functions individually, but they have to be designed such that the output of the map function can be accepted by the reduce function and the reduce function should be designed in such a way that it can accept the map output.

If you think in actual implementation terms, basically, the map function emitting outputs should match the data types accepted by reduce functions. You will understand this clearly when we see some code in our later chapters.

Data life cycle in the MapReduce framework

As we have discussed earlier, there is more to a MapReduce framework than just map and reduce functions. There is an input data division and accordingly the number of mappers are decided upon. Then, there are combiners, partitioners, and fling and sorting phase.

The following diagram depicts the data lifecycle from input to output via a MapReduce framework:

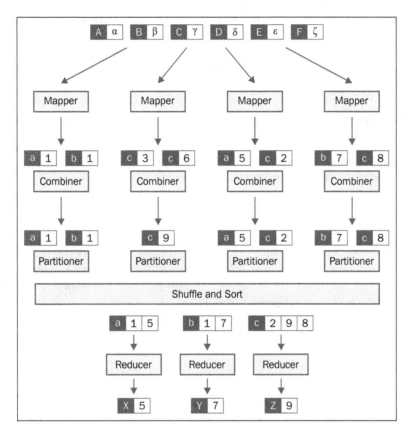

The following are the six distinct phases in the lifecycle of data being processed through the MapReduce framework:

- Creation of input splits
- Mapper
- Combiner
- Partitioner
- Shuffle and Sort
- Reducer

Creation of input data splits

In order to work on huge input datasets, subsets need to be created so that multiple mappers can be executed in parallel over those subsets. MapReduce frameworks have built-in features to take care of this. The responsibility of performing splits are generally with the **input formats**. Frameworks provide a bunch of predefined input formats, and if you need a custom way of splitting your dataset, you can also define your own input formats. If you do not want to split your input files, you can even configure that. There are configuration parameters provided by the framework dictating the maximum number of bytes to be present in a single split.

 Each input split is processed by one mapper. Hence, the number of mappers is equal to the number of input splits.

Record reader

Each split is further divided into multiple logical units to be processed by the user-defined map functions. That is, on each of these records, the map function will be executed once. Each input format has its implementation of a record reader. You may want to read line by line, that is, each line is a separate record. Or, you may want to process a paragraph at once with a single map function call; in such a case, your record reader should be capable of reading paragraphs as separate records, as shown in the following figure:

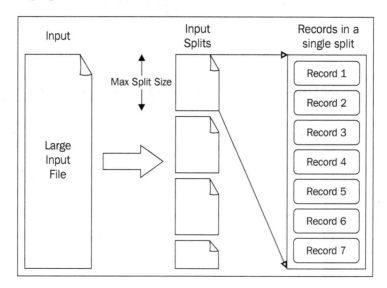

Mapper

Each map task processes a single split. The map tasks that are spawned by the framework to take on the task of executing map functions for each of the records of a single input split are fondly called as a Mapper. A map task is also entrusted to perform the tasks of combining and partitioning, which we will see in a while.

The following diagram shows the simplified data flow in the mapper phase:

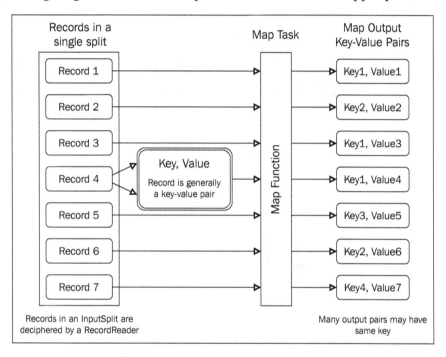

Combiner

You might call combiners to be mini-reducers. Use of combiners is optional and executed per map task. That is, there has to be a user-defined combine function that would be executed over all the output pairs of the map task. This function should be like a reduce function, that is, it should take in key and list of values as input parameter and emit one or more key-value pairs.

They are helpful in decreasing the effort that would go into the shuffle and sort phases later. Your mapper may be emitting more than one record per key, which would finally be grouped and passed to a single call of the `reducer` method. Hence, if these records can be combined even before passing them to reducers, the amount of data that will be shuffled across the network in order to get it to the right reducer will be reduced, resulting in better job performance. Also, reduction in the total amount of data to be sorted will lead to a quicker sorting.

 Unless you suspect that your map tasks are going to emit a considerable number of key-value pairs having the same key, you should not use a combiner. As combiners too take some execution time; hence, unless this extra time taken is justified by enough in-situ reductions by combiners, do not go for them. Also, keep in mind that combiners can be run multiple times by the framework.

The following diagram depicts the dataflow between mapper and combiner:

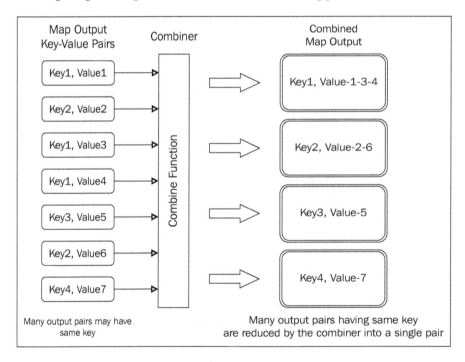

Partitioner

As map tasks running on different machines may produce output with the same keys that should be processed by a single reducer, there should be a way to decide upon map outputs with which key should be forwarded against which reducer for reduction.

The MapReduce framework has built-in capability to do this, which you can certainly customize. There is a partition function that helps the framework make the decision as to which reducer a given map output has to be forwarded.

Often, the default function is to get a numeric hash of the key and divide that by the total number of reducers, and allocate the output with that key to a reducer according to the remainder of the division. So, this function takes in the map output key and the total number of reducers as input parameters and emits an integer indicating the reducer to which that map output should be allocated for reduction.

This function in its simplest form will look like the following in Java if we consider that the map output key is of the KeyType (which in reality will be an actual data type):

```
int getPartition(KeyType key, int numberOfReducers){
  int hash=0;
  if(key!=null){
    hash = (key.toString().hashCode() ;
  }
  return (hash & Integer.MAX_VALUE) % numberOfReducers;
}
```

There are implementations of the partition function, wherein both the key and value are passed as input parameters along with total number of reducers.

Shuffle and sort

The map outputs with the same keys can be emitted by various map tasks running on separate machines. Now, as we have seen that using a partitioner, it is decided to which reducer a specific map output record will be sent. This process of moving around the map output records between different machines is called **shuffling**.

Each map task writes output to a memory buffer and spills the overflow data to a local disk in a round robin fashion. Now, before data is written to disk, the following operations take place:

1. The data is divided into partitions as per the partition function.

2. Within each partition, an in-memory sort is performed based on map output keys.

3. If a combiner function has been defined, it is executed over the sorted data for each of the partitions. This happens in memory only if the number of spills is less than a specific number, which is a configurable value in most of the frameworks and is generally a small integer such as 2 or 3.

Reducer

The number of reduce tasks are predefined, either you can explicitly tell the framework to have a certain number of reducers or the framework will decide it for you, but it will be decided from the onset of the job execution. This early decision helps in the distribution of map outputs among reducers.

Each map task has output data sorted and kept separately for each of the partitions. Basically, the map outputs are sorted and are present in containers tagged with the reducer that needs to do the reduction. Also, as there can be many map tasks that might have data for a particular reducer, a reduce task needs to perform the following operations:

1. Fetch the sorted map data from various machines having data for this reducer.

2. Merge that data.

3. Perform a sort operation.

4. Execute the reduce function over the sorted data in order.

The following diagram shows the dataflow between the mappers and reducers going through partitioning, sorting, and shuffling:

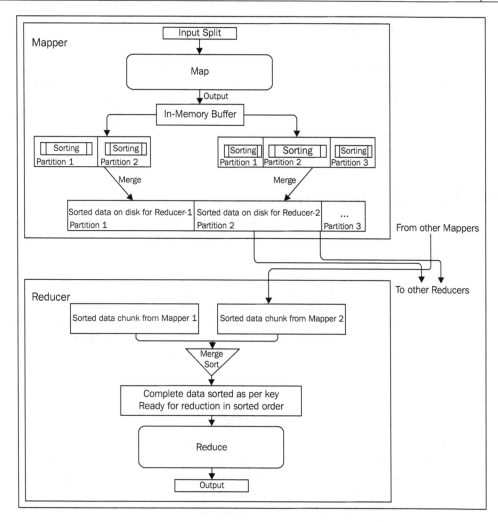

Real-world examples and use cases of MapReduce

Let's now check out a few of the actual applications using MapReduce. The MapReduce paradigm is the core of the distributed programming model in many applications to solve big data problems across different industries in the real world. There are many challenging problems such as log analytics, data analysis, recommendation engines, fraud detection, and user behavior analysis, among others, for which MapReduce is used as a solution.

Some of the examples of MapReduce usage are listed in the next sections.

Social networks

Most of us are daily users of sites such as Facebook, Twitter, and LinkedIn to connect with our friends, community, and colleagues. All of these sites are heavy users of the MapReduce model for solving problems such as who are the common friends/followers between you and another user on Facebook/Twitter or common connections in LinkedIn between two users. Many of the interesting features such as who visited your profile on LinkedIn or read your post on Facebook or Twitter can be computed using the MapReduce programming model.

Media and entertainment

Services such as Netflix and Hulu use Hadoop and MapReduce to solve problems such as finding out the most popular videos, what you might like based on what you have watched till now, or provide suggestions to newly signed up users based on their interests similar to existing users. Hadoop and MapReduce allow companies to identify user content consumption behavior and leverage insights to provide them with better suggestions so that they can increase the overall user engagement and revenue. We can use the MapReduce programming model to identify related videos for a given video using the meta of the video such as its category, cast or crew, and how users are watching videos in the system by analyzing the web logs and clickstream logs.

E-commerce and websites

Many of the e-commerce providers such as Amazon, Walmart, and eBay use the MapReduce programming model to identify popular products based on users' interests or purchasing behavior. These include building product recommendation engines for e-commerce catalogs by analyzing the website logs, purchase history, user interaction logs and so on. It can also be used to identify user sentiment for the given product by analyzing comments or reviews using MapReduce to identify the sentiment. Most of the leading e-commerce retailers have a very large inventory of the products in their systems, and it will be very difficult for users to discover all of them. So, building a recommendation engine or product suggestion engine can help drastically in providing related products based on user interests or their past purchase behavior.

The MapReduce programming model can also be used to analyze all search logs in the e-commerce website to identify what the most popular items are based on search and also identify which products are missing by analyzing all search logs.

Many website providers use the MapReduce model for analyzing the website logs to understand user visits, their engagement, locations, mobile devices and browsers used, and so on.

Fraud detection and financial analytics

Hadoop and MapReduce can be used in financial industries including companies such as banks, insurance providers, or payment gateways for fraud detection, identifying the trends, or business metrics by analyzing transactions and application logs. Let's take the example of an insurance company selling multiple products across different countries. They can capture all their transaction and application logs for processing using MapReduce to identify which are the most popular insurance products in different locations across the world. They can also identify the trend lines of newly launched products with respect to existing products and which products are purchased in groups by end users. Banks can analyze credit card spend data of their users to provide them with categorization of their spend and also make recommendations for different merchant offers by analyzing their anonymous purchase behavior over time.

Search engines and ad networks

Many popular search engine systems use MapReduce for understanding user behavior such as popular searches during a specific period or in a specific country or during a specific event such as presidential elections. It can be used to analyze and understand users' search behavior, trends, or missing results for specific keywords. Also, Adworks such as Yahoo! and InMobi use Hadoop and MapReduce for understanding ad impressions served, click-through rates, and user engagement behavior. It can be used to identify trends or popular publishers in their network.

ETL and data analytics

MapReduce programming can be used to migrate data, files, or records from one system to another using distributed models. Let's assume that we have 10 TB of files in DataCenter1 located in Europe and we want to migrate all these files to DataCenter2 located in the U.S. The traditional way of bulk copy and move will not work, so we can use the MapReduce programming model to build a distributed system for copying files from DataCenter1 to DataCenter2. We can use the map function to locate a specific file and break it down into chunks for transfer, while the reduce function can combine the chunks of a related file, perform checksum to ensure data integrity, and so on.

We can use MapReduce programming for analyzing large volumes of data from databases, data warehouses, or logs while implementing specific business logic to derive insights. It can also be for building **Extract, Transform, and Load** (ETL) systems for moving data from one data store to an other.

> One of the most important issues to understand while performing data analysis using the MapReduce model is to be aware of the different data privacy and safeguarding laws of different countries. In most countries, the local laws mandate to safeguard end user privacy by using anonymous user data for any further analysis or analytics. This subject is out of scope in this book, but it's important to be aware of local data privacy laws before collecting, aggregating, and analyzing data.

Software distributions built on the MapReduce framework

One of the most popular software distributions made for large-scale distributed computing based on the MapReduce framework is Apache Hadoop.

There are many other distributions that use Apache Hadoop as their base and repackage it with additional features and improvements. The most popular among them are listed as follows:

- Cloudera Distribution
- MapR

Apache Hadoop

Apache Hadoop is a platform for big data storage and processing. It is the most popular open source implementation of the MapReduce framework. It is an Apache top-level project and is widely used for many big data problems.

As it is available under Apache license 2.0, it has been taken as the backbone over which many other custom and improved distributions have been created.

We will learn about Apache Hadoop in greater detail in the next chapter. We will also use Apache Hadoop with Amazon EMR.

MapR

MapR is a derived implementation of Apache Hadoop claiming improved performance and full data protection. It provides its distributions in three different flavors: M3, M5, and M7. While M3 is a free version, the other two have some added features and come with some cost.

Along with Apache Hadoop, Amazon EMR also provides the option to launch your cluster with one of the MapR distributions and charges you accordingly.

Cloudera distribution

Cloudera distribution of Apache Hadoop (CDH) is an open source distribution. Basically, Cloudera is a company that provides services and support to enterprise-level implementation of Hadoop based systems. Its main product is Cloudera Manager that helps in the administration of enterprise big data solutions. Cloudera is one of the largest contributors to Apache Hadoop.

Summary

We learned about the very popular MapReduce framework in this chapter. We covered the basics of MapReduce style of programming along with the architectural data flow that happens in any MapReduce framework.

We did not talk about the network architecture, which includes concepts such as JobTracker and TaskTracker. We will learn about these and more in the next chapter where we will take up Apache Hadoop and its architecture in detail.

3
Apache Hadoop

Very few people will deny that the evolution of Apache Hadoop has been one of the major driving forces behind the advancements we see in Big Data processing. Apache Hadoop has enabled businesses of all sizes to start getting more out of their data. It has not only helped businesses get more from their data, but has also been very useful in the field of medicine and healthcare—resulting in better lives for many. From fraud detection by financial institutions to providing recommendations to users by an e-commerce portal, Apache Hadoop has revolutionized the industry in many ways.

What is Apache Hadoop?

It is an open source software framework that enables reliable and scalable storage and processing of large datasets in a distributed environment.

Here is the definition provided on the official Apache Hadoop's website:

> *"The Apache Hadoop software library is a framework that allows for the distributed processing of large data sets across clusters of computers using simple programming models. It is designed to scale up from single servers to thousands of machines, each offering local computation and storage. Rather than rely on hardware to deliver high-availability, the library itself is designed to detect and handle failures at the application layer, so delivering a highly-available service on top of a cluster of computers, each of which may be prone to failures."*

It has been designed to handle hardware-level failures at the application layer itself, and this is one of the prime features that enables use of commodity hardware as part of the clusters crunching data using Apache Hadoop. It provides the ability to scale the running cluster as per the requirement.

The founder of Hadoop, Doug Cutting, had initially designed it to solve the need to store and compute large numbers of files that were generated from Apache Nutch, an open source web search engine. Apache Nutch, which we can say was the root of Hadoop, was a subproject of Apache Lucene, a text search library created by Doug Cutting himself.

When Doug Cutting, the chief architect of the curiously named Hadoop, was creating this open source software, he knew that the project would need an appropriate name. Fortunately, he had one up his sleeve that he had saved for an appropriate time. Thanks to his son who, while playing with his yellow elephant toy, coined the term Hadoop for the first time!

It has been primarily built on two of the papers from Google, namely, Google MapReduce and **Google File System (GFS)**. It has gone through a series of improvements since its first release that involved the addition of a robust job scheduling and resource management framework. It provides the complete package, having a viable solution to a large amount of data storage as well as data analysis on that stored data.

The name Apache Hadoop, sometimes, is also used for the family of projects related to distributed computing and Big Data processing, most of which are hosted by Apache Software Foundation. The Hadoop ecosystem, as it has come to be called, is growing with many projects coming up that complement Hadoop or use Hadoop.

Hadoop modules

An Apache Hadoop project mainly comprises the following four components:

- **Hadoop Common**: This module comprises the common utilities that provide the basic support to other Hadoop modules. This includes the components and implementations for the common I/O operations and utilities to handle the distributed filesystem. It has implementations of abstraction over Java RPC and serialization required to be used in other Hadoop modules.

- **Hadoop Distributed File System**: This is an implementation of a distributed filesystem that enables storage of large amounts of data in redundancy over a cluster of commodity machines, providing high aggregate throughput access to data. Its implementation has been inspired by a paper published by Google on its proprietary, distributed filesystem named GFS.

- **Hadoop YARN**: With the initial implementation of Hadoop, the MapReduce module itself took care of both cluster resource management as well as the actual data processing. With Hadoop 2.0, a new framework was introduced that takes care of the cluster resource management and job scheduling tasks. This framework is called YARN.

- **Hadoop MapReduce**: With Hadoop 2.0, it is now a YARN-based system for distributed processing of large scale data. Hence, this module named Hadoop MapReduce is basically the implementation of the programming model we discussed in the previous chapter, and it forms the core component of Apache Hadoop. Its implementation too has been inspired by a paper published by Google on the MapReduce framework for distributed computing on commodity hardware.

Hadoop Distributed File System

The **Hadoop Distributed File System (HDFS)** is a distributed filesystem that has been designed to run on commodity hardware. It excels in availability, scalability, and fault tolerance. It is suitable for applications that need to process large datasets with high throughput access. HDFS was originally built as the storage framework for Apache Nutch, which is a web search engine project.

Major architectural goals of HDFS

As HDFS has been designed to solve storage problems with large datasets, it has been built with the following major assumptions and architectural goals in mind:

- **Hardware will fail**: Hardware failure is a norm rather than an exception. A deployment of HDFS may have multiple servers, hundreds or even thousands, each storing a part of data present in the filesystem as a whole. Now, at any given point of time, it is very likely that out of many servers, some are nonfunctional. Therefore, detection of such faults and quick, automatic recovery from them is a core architectural goal of HDFS.

- **Emphasis on high throughput of data access over low latency of data access**: HDFS has been designed to be able to provide streaming access of data to the applications using it. So basically, it hasn't been designed for general purpose applications, wherein there is an interactive use by the user. It has been designed for batch processing. It can be said that HDFS isn't POSIX-compliant, as it relaxes few of the POSIX requirements in order to achieve high throughput for data access by the target applications.

- **Tuned to support large files**: HDFS has been built to support applications having to deal with large files. A file in HDFS is expected to be of gigabytes to terabytes in size. It has been designed to be able to support tens of millions of files on a single HDFS instance having the capability to scale to hundreds of nodes, and hence, providing high aggregate data bandwidth to its applications. In fact, HDFS performs rather poorly if large numbers of small files are stored in it.

- **It has a write-once-read-many access model for files**: This is called the Simple Coherence Model. This basically means that there is no append feature available once a file had been created, written to, and closed. This does simplify data coherency issues, especially in a distributed environment, and ultimately contributes to high throughput data access. The official document states that there is a plan to support appending-writes to files in the future.

- **Portable across heterogeneous hardware and software platforms**:

Moving computation is cheaper than moving data

This is one of the simple architectural principles on which Apache Hadoop has built its computation allocation strategy. Over the years, computation and storage got cheaper, but network and disk speeds didn't really catch up. Hence, a computation requested to be done over a large dataset will be more efficient if it is performed near to where data resides physically. This approach is better than moving data over the network. This results in minimizing network communication and effectively reducing traffic and increasing the overall throughput of the system. HDFS has built-in capabilities that applications can use to move themselves closer to where the data is located.

Block replication and rack awareness

HDFS is designed to allow applications to move processing of data to where data resides physically or to a relatively nearer location. In order to achieve this, HDFS breaks files into blocks as per its configurable block size and replicates these blocks into a number of different servers according to a configurable replication factor. The default block size is 128 MB and the default replication factor is 3.

HDFS instances are often run over large clusters composed of many servers spread across multiple racks. The rack awareness feature aims at achieving higher fault tolerance in order to cater to the situations wherein a complete rack fails. HDFS is designed to distribute data evenly between different racks in order to provide faster access and making it more fault tolerant. This is one feature that other distributed filesystems do not have.

Let's assume that we have a file of 300 MB and we have the default HDFS configuration, that is 128 MB block size and a replication factor of 3. Hence, the file will be divided into three blocks; let's name them for simplicity as follows:

- Block A (128 MB)
- Block B (128 MB)
- Block C (44 MB)

 Even though Block C is 44 MB in size, storing it in HDFS will take only 44 MB space and not the whole 128 MB of block size.

Now, let's say we have two racks of data storage available, namely **Rack-I** and **Rack-II**, and each rack has two data nodes each. HDFS would store the aforementioned blocks in the following fashion:

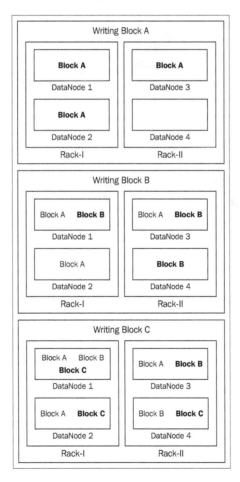

Since our replication factor is 3, each data block will be written into three different data nodes. Now, HDFS makes sure that at least one copy of the data block exists in both the racks. In order to achieve that, after writing **Block A** in one of the data nodes in **Rack-I**, HDFS copies it to one of the data nodes in **Rack-II** and from there in a round robin fashion, and as per the availability of space in each of the data nodes, all other blocks are written.

Here is what the official documentation states regarding the replica placement policy in HDFS:

> *"For the common case, when the replication factor is three, HDFS's placement policy is to put one replica on one node in the local rack, another on a different node in the local rack, and the last on a different node in a different rack. This policy cuts the inter-rack write traffic which generally improves write performance. The chance of rack failure is far less than that of node failure; this policy does not impact data reliability and availability guarantees. However, it does reduce the aggregate network bandwidth used when reading data since a block is placed in only two unique racks rather than three. With this policy, the replicas of a file do not evenly distribute across the racks. One third of replicas are on one node, two thirds of replicas are on one rack, and the other third are evenly distributed across the remaining racks. This policy improves write performance without compromising data reliability or read performance."*

The HDFS architecture

HDFS has a master-slave architecture. An HDFS cluster consists of a single master called the **NameNode**, which manages the filesystem namespace for the entire distributed filesystem and also controls the file access. Additionally, there are multiple **DataNodes**, usually one per node in the cluster. Each DataNode manages storage attached to the node it is running on.

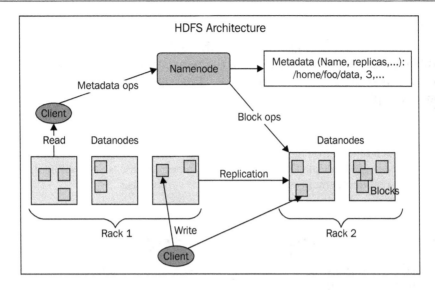

NameNode

NameNode is the arbitrator and central repository of file namespace in the cluster. The NameNode executes the primary filesystem namespace operations such as opening, closing, and renaming files and directories. It also determines the mapping of blocks to DataNodes, as it holds the metadata about all the block replicas and location of their respective DataNodes.

NameNode keeps track of the health of each of the DataNodes in the cluster via a periodic heartbeat, which it receives from each DataNode. A proper periodic heartbeat informs NameNode that data in the DataNode is ready for use. If there are no recent heartbeats, the NameNode assumes that the specific DataNode is dead and updates its metadata accordingly. It does not forward any further I/O requests to that DataNode. Death of a DataNode brings down the replication factor for the blocks available in that node from their specified values. NameNode keeps track of this and constantly initiates new replication in other DataNodes for those blocks.

Prior to Hadoop 2, NameNode was the **Single Point of Failure (SPOF)** for an HDFS cluster. With Hadoop 2, the addition of HDFS High Availability feature allows running of two redundant NameNodes in the same cluster in an active/passive configuration with a hot standby. As NameNode stores huge metadata in RAM, it is advisable to use a machine with good hardware and lots of RAM as NameNode.

DataNode

DataNode manages the storage attached to the node on which it runs. It is responsible for serving all the read and write requests. It also performs certain operations on instruction from NameNode. These operations include creation, deletion, and replication of blocks.

 In a typical deployment, NameNode is run on a dedicated machine. Each of the other machines in the cluster runs one instance of DataNode. Running multiple DataNodes on the same machine isn't prohibited, but in a real deployment scenario, such a case rarely arises.

Apache Hadoop MapReduce

Apache Hadoop MapReduce is the most popular implementation of the MapReduce programming paradigm. Coupled with a distributed storage framework in the form of HDFS, it provides a very robust system for processing of large datasets over a cluster of hundreds or even thousands of nodes.

The Hadoop MapReduce project can be broken down into the following three major components:

- **The MapReduce API**: This includes the set of libraries available for the end users to create their applications. You will use these to create the `map` and `reduce` functions to be executed by the framework. The APIs also have provisions to set various configurations for the cluster and its components.

- **The MapReduce framework**: This is the runtime implementation of various phases involved in the execution of a MapReduce task, which includes the map phase, sort/shuffle/merge phase, and the reduce phase. The intricacies of the data flow throughout various stages form the major part of this component.

- **The MapReduce cluster management system**: This consists of the backend system that manages the complete infrastructure to execute your MapReduce applications. It includes the cluster resource management along with the scheduling of jobs submitted to the cluster.

Having this separation of concerns enables users to focus only on the creation of their application, letting the Hadoop framework take care of the data flow and resource management in order to get the task executed.

Hadoop MapReduce 1.x

Hadoop 0.20.205, having matured enough, has been renamed as Hadoop 1.0 to be consistent with the naming of other enterprise products. It is also called **MRv1**.

The following diagram shows the MapReduce 1.0 framework architecture:

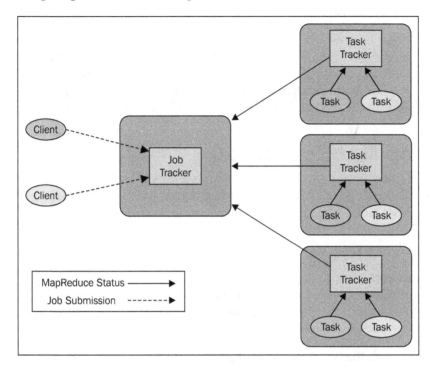

JobTracker

JobTracker is responsible for managing the cluster resources. It is also responsible to identify the TaskTracker most suitable to execute a given task. When a new job is submitted to JobTracker, it first breaks the job into multiple tasks as per the input data; for that, it connects with NameNode to identify the list of DataNodes and blocks where the input data for the submitted job resides. Now, JobTracker allocates those tasks to respective TaskTrackers accordingly.

In this architecture, JobTracker is the master, while each of the TaskTrackers acts like its slave. A heartbeat signal between JobTracker and TaskTracker is the time when JobTracker passes information to TaskTracker to execute. If JobTracker hasn't received any recent heartbeat, it deems TaskTracker to be dead and stops allocating any further tasks to it. Also, it tries to schedule the tasks being done by the dead TaskTracker with other alive TaskTrackers.

TaskTracker

TaskTracker, being a slave, follows orders from its master, JobTracker. It launches or stops tasks when asked to do so from the JobTracker. It also has the responsibility of sending periodic status updates to the JobTracker regarding the task it is running. TaskTrackers are normally configured in such a way that they can occupy one CPU core per TaskTracker.

Some tasks may be slower than others due to various reasons including hardware or software issues. Since tasks are run in parallel, the overall time taken depends on the slowest task. So, if Hadoop detects a slow running task, it launches another equivalent task. This is called as **speculative execution**. The task which completes first announces its completion, and Hadoop kills the other one as it's no longer required.

Hadoop MapReduce 2.0

Hadoop MapReduce underwent a sort of complete overhaul with its Hadoop 0.23 version. This version is now commonly known as MapReduce 2.0, MapReduce NextGen, MRv2, or YARN.

Hadoop YARN

We saw earlier that Hadoop MapReduce can be seen as composed of three distinct components. One of these, the cluster management system has been now decoupled in the form of a subproject under Apache Hadoop, named **YARN** (short for **Yet Another Resource Negotiator**).

Now with MRv2, the responsibilities of job scheduling and resource management will no longer be part of the MapReduce implementation. The component of MapReduce that was responsible for those tasks has been carved out as a more generic module that will provide Apache Hadoop's robust distributed computing infrastructure to be used along with many other different types of data processing layers in addition to that of MapReduce.

With the Hadoop 1.x architecture, JobTracker being a single point of task distribution, didn't allow for scaling out of the cluster to a very large size without performance issues.

The following diagram shows the high-level difference between MRv1 and MRv2:

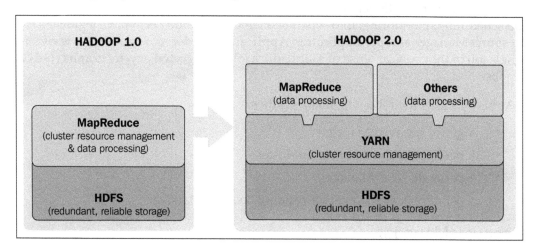

How does YARN work?

The following diagram shows the MapReduce 2.0 (YARN) framework architecture:

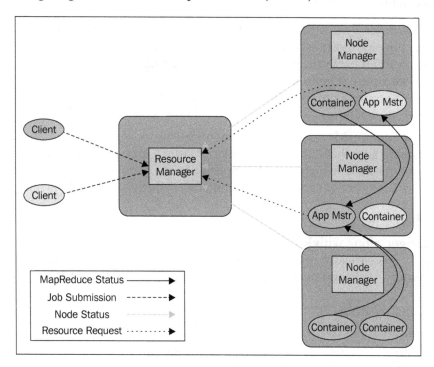

As the official documentation states, the fundamental idea of MRv2 is to split up the two major functionalities of the JobTracker, resource management and job scheduling/monitoring, into separate daemons. The idea is to have a global **ResourceManager** and per-application **ApplicationMaster**. An application is either a single job in the classical sense of MapReduce jobs or **directed acyclic graphs (DAG)** of jobs.

YARN consists of the following major entities:

- A global ResourceManager
- A per-application ApplicationMaster
- A per-node NodeManager
- A per-application Container running on NodeManager

ResourceManager

The **ResourceManager (RM)** is the ultimate authority on allocation of resources among all the applications in the system.

It has two main components:

- **Scheduler**: This is responsible for allocating required resources to various running applications according to various constraints of need and available capacity. It performs no monitoring or tracking of application status, and is hence a **pure scheduler**. It performs scheduling based on the abstract notion of a resource **Container** that incorporates elements such as memory, CPU, disk, and network, among others; as of now, only memory is supported.

- **ApplicationsManager**: This is responsible for accepting job submissions and making sure that it gets a Container to launch an ApplicationMaster for the submitted job, which would be specific to the submitted job application. It also takes care of restarting the Container, which has the ApplicationMaster.

NodeManager

NodeManager, along with ResourceManager, forms the data computation framework. It is basically a reporter that reports the usage of resource capacity (CPU, memory, disk, and network) by the containers on the node it runs.

ApplicationMaster

Every application has its own instance of **ApplicationMaster (AM)**. It has the responsibility of negotiating the required resources from ResourceManager. It also works with one or more NodeManagers to execute and monitor tasks.

Container

A Container represents a successful resource allocation from ResourceManager. A Container grants rights to an application for usage of a specific amount of resources on a specific host. Now, it's the responsibility of ApplicationMaster to present the Container to the NodeManager of the node for which the Container has been allotted and acquired access to the resources.

The benefits of having YARN in the Hadoop backyard:

- **Enhanced scalability**: Having a dedicated ResourceManager focusing exclusively on scheduling, it can manage a large cluster with much ease.
- **Improved cluster utilization**: ResourceManager is a pure scheduler that optimizes cluster utilization according to various criteria such as capacity guarantees and fairness in resource allocation.
- **Allowed support for processing engines other than MapReduce**: Additional programming models such as graph processing and iterative modeling are now possible to be plugged-in in place of MapReduce for data processing.

So, now YARN takes the distributed resource management and scheduling capabilities that were in MapReduce 1.x and packages them into a separate module altogether so that these capabilities can be used by new processing engines. This also enables the MapReduce project to now focus and grow further into its core functionality, that is, to efficiently process distributed data—leaving the cluster resource management responsibilities with YARN.

If you have already created applications on MRv1 and want to use MRv2, don't be discouraged, as MRv2 maintains backward API compatibility with the previous stable release (MRv1). This means that all MapReduce jobs should still run unchanged on top of MRv2 with just a recompile.

Apache Hadoop as a platform

Apache Hadoop is generally also referred to as a family of Hadoop-related projects. It is also commonly known as **Hadoop Ecosystem**. This includes some of the datastores created on top of HDFS and some having created abstraction layers on top of Hadoop MapReduce.

Right now, as listed on Apache Hadoop's official website, the following projects are part of this family:

- **Ambari**: A web-based management tool for Hadoop clusters
- **Avro**: A data serialization system
- **Cassandra**: A scalable multimaster datastore capable of storing large datasets
- **Chukwa**: A distributed data collection engine
- **HBase**: A scalable, distributed database
- **Hive**: A data warehouse engine built on top of Hadoop MapReduce with SQL such as ad hoc querying
- **Mahout**: A scalable machine learning library built on top of Hadoop MapReduce
- **Pig**: A high-level programming language providing an abstraction over Hadoop
- **Spark**: A fast and general engine for large-scale data processing
- **Tez**: A generalized dataflow programming framework, built on Hadoop YARN
- **ZooKeeper**: A high-performance coordination service for distributed applications

Let's now discuss two of the most popular projects of the Hadoop family in brief.

Apache Pig

Pig is a high-level programming language that runs over Hadoop. It was originally designed and developed by Yahoo! in 2006 and later on moved to Apache in 2007. The motive behind designing Pig was to allow the developers to focus more on analyzing the problem statement involving large datasets and spend less time writing the MapReduce jobs.

Pig comprises of two components: one is the scripting language, PigLatin, and the other one is the runtime environment where the script executes. PigLatin is a dataflow language describing how the data will be transformed at different stages. On runtime, the operations in the PigLatin script are converted to the series of MapReduce jobs, which are run by the Hadoop clusters. Although Pig has limited defined operators, we can extend and write our own functions, categorized as the **User Defined Functions (UDFs)**.

Pig has gained tremendous popularity, especially in the field of research. It helps researchers to create the best working prototype by providing a quick benchmark for their analysis or algorithms. Pig, with its services such as ETL Data Pipelines, has also proved to be very useful in cases where there is a requirement for iterative data processing and data analysis.

Apache Hive

Hive is a powerful data warehouse package that is built on top of Hadoop. It helps keep analysts and developers busy accessing Hadoop Data, hence justifying the name "Hive". Since Pig was a new framework and required more efforts in grasping the same, Hive was developed by Facebook for the SQL developers to take advantage of Hadoop without any additional learning.

Hive allows users to explore, structure, and analyze the data stored in the Hadoop clusters by writing in **Hive Query Language** (**HQL**), which is mainly inspired by SQL. Like SQL, you can exploit the HQL in various forms such as through command line (Hive Shell) or even a database client known as Hive Thrift, which can easily be integrated with the other programming languages. Even JDBC or ODBC drivers allow playing with Hive data. Each HQL query is broken down into a series of MapReduce jobs that run over Hadoop clusters.

As Hive runs over Hadoop, it has several limitations as well. Due to the high latency time for the queries, they cannot be used in real-time systems. It doesn't support row-level insertion, deletion, and update operations. However, despite these limited features, it is a very useful tool in the field of text mining, collaborative filtering, predictive modeling, and even document indexing.

If you know SQL, Hive will look familiar to you. However, you have to rely on Hive optimizer to optimize your queries. While Pig requires more verbose coding, it provides you more control over optimization and dataflow than Hive does.

Summary

In this chapter, we learned about the components of Apache Hadoop in detail, along with their architecture. We also saw the major enhancement brought into Hadoop in the form of YARN and how it opens up many possibilities for Apache Hadoop to be used as the underlying engine for distributed computing by various different programming layers in place of MapReduce.

We will now move on to discovering Amazon Elastic MapReduce in greater depth in our next chapter, learning to program on Hadoop and executing the same on EMR.

4
Amazon EMR – Hadoop on Amazon Web Services

The goal of this chapter is to introduce you to AWS **Elastic MapReduce (EMR)** and show its advantages over in-house Hadoop clusters.

Traditionally, very few companies had access to large-scale infrastructure to build Big Data applications. However, cloud computing has democratized the access to infrastructure allowing developers and companies to quickly perform new experiments without worrying about the need for setting up or scaling infrastructure.

As we have seen in *Chapter 1*, *Amazon Web Services*, a cloud provides an infrastructure as a service platform to allow businesses to build applications and host them reliably with scalable infrastructure. It includes a variety of application-level services to help developers to accelerate their development and deployment times. Amazon EMR is one of the hosted services provided by AWS and is built on top of a scalable AWS infrastructure to build Big Data applications.

What is AWS EMR?

Amazon EMR provides a hosted Hadoop, Pig, Hive, and HBase services for developers and businesses to help them build Big Data applications without worrying about the deployment complexity or managing Hadoop clusters with underlying infrastructure. Many improvements have been made into the open source Apache Hadoop and other applications in order to make them interact seamlessly with other AWS services.

Features of EMR

Let's now discuss some of the key features of EMR, most of which come with EMR being a service provided over cloud infrastructure. These are the features that are hard to achieve on an in-house local cluster:

- **Ease of use**: EMR provides a hosted Hadoop service without worrying about deployment complexity or configuration challenges. We can use multiple Hadoop distributions and third-party libraries with EMR. We can easily integrate EMR with other AWS services such as S3, DynamoDB, Redshift, CloudWatch, and many more.

- **Elasticity**: EMR allows you to scale up and scale down the nodes in a Hadoop cluster without worrying about underlying infrastructure. You can easily launch a cluster with a few nodes or thousands of nodes in a matter of minutes.

- **Scalable storage**: You can use AWS S3 as a filesystem with EMR, which is scalable to petabytes of storage. We don't need to worry about managing the filesystem for our applications or underlying failures of disks. You can be rest assured about not losing your data if you use S3 as the final output location of your Hadoop tasks.

- **Cost effective**: EMR allows us to leverage their spot pricing for EMR to build large-scale clusters at a lower cost. With EMR, we can quickly launch a five-node cluster to analyze data for a few hours at the cost of less than $1. It also gives you the ability to start with a small number of nodes and increase them on the fly when the need arises. For example, you might want to speed up the process or when after completion of a small task, you want to process another task using the same cluster that needs more nodes to finish within a stipulated time. This effectively reduces your cost.

- **Configurable**: EMR provides a custom bootstrapping capability to override default configurations or packages. You have complete control over the cluster and can get root access to underlying instances in the EMR cluster to make any required changes. It's also easy to use various third-party tools with EMR as AWS provides configuration and customization options. You can also use monitoring tools such as Ganglia along with your EMR cluster.

- **Programmable**: This is one feature of AWS that makes it easy to build custom application layers on top of its services. EMR provides API and client SDK to programmatically create and manage clusters. You can programmatically increase or decrease the existing cluster to leverage AWS spot pricing to reduce your costs. You can monitor your running jobs and raise alerts such as e-mails by writing an application using APIs and SDKs provided by AWS.

Before accessing the EMR service from Amazon, you will need to subscribe to it from the AWS web console. Once you have subscribed to the EMR service, you can use the AWS web console, API SDK, or CLI tools to launch and manage EMR clusters.

We will learn about this in more detail in *Chapter 6*, *Executing Hadoop Jobs on an Amazon EMR Cluster*, where we will launch an EMR cluster via the AWS console.

Accessing Amazon EMR features

Once you have subscribed to the AWS EMR service, it can be accessed in multiple ways:

- **Web console**: This is a web interface to access all AWS offerings. You can use the **EMR** section within the web console to launch EMR jobs and manage them.

- **SDK**: EMR provides SDKs that have functions to access EMR features using popular languages such as Java, Python, .NET, and many more. You can launch, manage, or customize EMR clusters using SDK.

- **CLI tool**: This is a client-side tool that can be installed on your computer to access EMR services and manage the jobs via command line. This is a client written in Ruby. We will read about it in detail in *Chapter 8*, *Amazon EMR – Command-line Interface Client*.

- **WebService API**: Amazon provides low-level API access to EMR features for custom integration or to build a specific toolkit for your business needs.

Programming on AWS EMR

Hadoop allows you to write programs using a variety of languages such as C++, Java, Python, Ruby, PHP, Perl, Node.js, R, Hive, and Pig Latin. You can refer to the AWS EMR documentation at `http://aws.amazon.com/articles/Elastic-MapReduce` for sample applications.

Let's now discuss the various ways in which you can program your solutions over Amazon EMR. When you add a job step to be executed on an EMR cluster, you will have to choose from the following options. This will let EMR know your programming choice and accordingly set up the execution environment:

- **Custom JAR**: For programmers familiar with the Java language, Hadoop supports writing applications using Custom JAR in Java. For writing Hadoop applications using Custom JAR, we need to be familiar with MapReduce APIs and Java programming. It allows customization of the underlying functionalities as they are exposed as APIs for programmers to override the default behavior. We can also use the cascading Java library.

 If you are comfortable with Java as a programming language, then going for the custom JAR way of creating a solution is always recommended. Using Java gives you much more control over the various functions as Apache Hadoop is written in Java and you can override and customize many default behaviors to suit your requirements.

- **Streaming Hadoop**: EMR supports the usage of Hadoop streaming to write MapReduce jobs quickly using any scripting language. You can write jobs using Ruby, PHP, or Python without worrying about the underlying Hadoop APIs. However, using Hadoop streaming limits you to only being a user of the APIs while creating your solutions. You should use this way of programming as a solution over EMR when you don't have familiarity with Java and also when you have relatively less time to create a solution, when a scripting language such as Python or Ruby with minimal codes is a better choice.

- **Apache Hive**: Amazon EMR supports Hive to allow developers or business analysts to quickly write applications using a familiar SQL style syntax. A Hive query is broken down into multiple MapReduce tasks and executed.

  According to Apache Hive's official website, `hive.apache.org`:

  > *"The Apache Hive™ data warehouse software facilitates querying and managing large datasets residing in distributed storage. Hive provides a mechanism to project structure onto this data and query the data using a SQL-like language called HiveQL. At the same time this language also allows traditional map/reduce programmers to plug in their custom mappers and reducers when it is inconvenient or inefficient to express this logic in HiveQL."*

So, if you are someone who is more comfortable with SQLs and aren't very familiar with programming languages, this should be your choice of programming your Big Data solutions on EMR.

- **Apache Pig**: Pig is a high-level scripting language for writing data analysis applications over a large volume of data. Pig has a compiler which in turn translates Pig jobs into MapReduce programs by abstracting the complexity from end users.

The EMR architecture

Let's get familiar with the EMR architecture and concepts before we get to writing a Hadoop program and executing that using EMR. This section outlines the key concepts of EMR.

Hadoop offers distributed processing by using the MapReduce framework for execution of tasks on a set of servers or compute nodes (also known as a cluster). One of the nodes in the Hadoop cluster will be controlling the distribution of tasks to other nodes and it's called the **Master Node**. The nodes executing the tasks using MapReduce are called **Slave Nodes**:

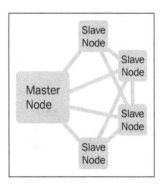

Amazon EMR is designed to work with many other AWS services such as S3 for input/output data storage, DynamoDB, and Redshift for output data. EMR uses AWS CloudWatch metrics to monitor the cluster performance and raise notifications for user-specified alarms. We can create on-demand Hadoop clusters using EMR while storing the input and output data in S3 without worrying about managing a 24*7 cluster or HDFS for data storage.

The Amazon EMR job flow is shown in the following diagram:

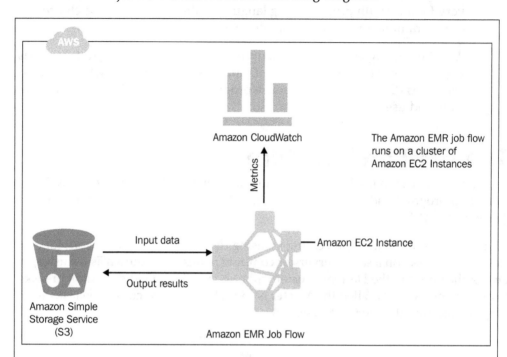

Types of nodes

Amazon EMR provides three different roles for the servers or nodes in the cluster and they map to the Hadoop roles of master and slave nodes. When you create an EMR cluster, then it's called a **Job Flow**, which has been created to execute a set of jobs or job steps one after the other. We will learn more about Job Flows and **Steps** in a later section. The following are the types of nodes:

- **Master node**: This node controls and manages the cluster. It distributes the MapReduce tasks to nodes in the cluster and monitors the status of task execution. Every EMR cluster will have only one master node in a master instance group.

- **Core nodes**: These nodes will execute MapReduce tasks and provide HDFS for storing the data related to task execution. The EMR cluster will have core nodes as part of it in a core instance group. The core node is related to the slave node in Hadoop. So, basically these nodes have two-fold responsibility: the first one is to execute the map and reduce tasks allocated by the master and the second is to hold the data blocks.

- **Task nodes**: These nodes are used for only MapReduce task execution and they are optional while launching the EMR cluster. The task node is related to the slave node in Hadoop and is part of a task instance group in EMR.

> When you scale down your clusters, you cannot remove any core nodes. This is because EMR doesn't want to let you lose your data blocks. You can remove nodes from a task group while scaling down your cluster.
>
> You should also be using only task instance groups to have spot instances, as spot instances can be taken away as per your bid price and you would not want to lose your data blocks.

You can launch a cluster having just one node, that is, with just one master node and no other nodes. In that case, the same node will act as both master and core nodes. For simplicity, you can assume a node as EC2 server in EMR.

EMR Job Flow and Steps

A Job Flow is a user-defined action for executing a set of related Job Steps using an EMR cluster. A MapReduce program will be referred to as a Job Step in EMR and it can be written using one of the approaches specified in the *Programming on AWS EMR* section.

A Job Flow typically consists of one or more Job Steps, where output from one Job Step becomes an input to the next Job Step with data being shared across Job Steps using HDFS. The data will be stored in HDFS as long as the EMR cluster is running and, upon termination, the data will be lost. So, if we are running transient clusters, then the final Job Step should store the output data in a S3 bucket.

When you are creating a Job Flow with multiple Job Steps, then each of those Job Steps will be executed in the sequential order of their addition to the Job Flow. The maximum number of Job Steps in an EMR cluster is 256; however, this may change in the future.

Job Steps

A Job Step is a unit of work and it can be an application of one of the following types:

- Custom JAR
- A streaming program
- A Hive program
- A Pig program

Each Job Step will be executed one or more times until it succeeds or fails.

Let's say we want to perform web access log processing using EMR to understand top URLs, HTTP status codes, IP addresses, and so on. Then, we will create a Job Flow with multiple Job Steps as outlined in the following bullet list to do different tasks, all in sequence. Each step is like a logical successor to the previous one and requires the previous one to have completed successfully:

- **Job Step 1**: This provides access and cleans the input logs
- **Job Step 2**: This analyzes the logs after cleaning by URL, HTTP status code, and IP address
- **Job Step 3**: This creates summary reports based on URLs, HTTP status codes, or IP addresses

At any given point of time in the life cycle of a Job Step, it will have one of the following states:

- **RUNNING**
- **COMPLETED**
- **PENDING**
- **FAILED**
- **CANCELLED**

In an EMR cluster, you can track the status of each Job Step in a Job Flow using WebConsole or CLI tools.

What if the Job Step fails?

Generally, if one of the Job Steps fails, then all the subsequent pending Job Steps should be marked with the **CANCELLED** state. However, EMR lets you control this as well; you can set the action to be performed if the step fails.
This can be done while adding a Job Step.

EMR provides the following three choices:

- **Continue**: If you are creating a Job Flow which has disjointed Job Steps, that is, a Job Flow in which it is alright to execute a step even if the previous one has failed, then in that case, you should set Continue to be your action on failure.

- **Cancel and wait**: This will be the option you would choose most often. If you want your cluster to cancel all the already added steps, which are in the queue and are yet to be executed when one of the steps failed, then you would set `Cancel` and wait to be your action on failure. If this behavior has been set for a step, then after a step has failed and all the added steps are cancelled, you can add fresh steps and their processing will start immediately in the order of their execution.

  Let's assume that you have three Job Steps and for all the steps, we have selected `Cancel and wait`. Initially, the states for each step will be as follows:

  ```
  Job Step1 - RUNNING
  Job Step2 - PENDING
  Job Step3 - PENDING
  ```

  Now, say if `Job Step1` fails, the states will be as follows:

  ```
  Job Step1 - FAILED
  Job Step2 - CANCELLED
  Job Step3 - CANCELLED
  ```

  Your cluster will be still running if you have launched your cluster with **keep alive** enabled. You will then quickly find out the reason for the failure of step 1, fix it, and add the job steps again. Now, the Job steps list along with their states will look as follows:

  ```
  Job Step1 - FAILED
  Job Step2 - CANCELLED
  Job Step3 - CANCELLED
  Job Step1 - RUNNING
  Job Step2 - PENDING
  Job Step3 - PENDING
  ```

- **Terminate cluster**: If you are creating a cluster, which isn't going to be monitored actively and you do not want to either continue or cancel and wait when one of the job steps fails, in that case, you should choose to set `Terminate cluster` to be your action on failure.

The following diagram illustrates the status of Job Steps in a typical Job Flow in EMR.

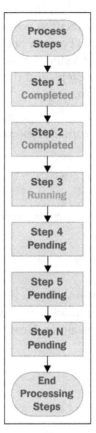

An EMR cluster

The Job Steps of a Job Flow are executed using an EMR cluster. You can think of an EMR cluster as a set of servers running on the AWS platform.

An EMR cluster may have one of the following states:

- **STARTING**
- **BOOTSTRAPPING**
- **RUNNING**
- **WAITING**
- **SHUTTING_DOWN**
- **TERMINATED**
- **COMPLETED**
- **FAILED**

When we launch an EMR cluster, it will be in the **STARTING** state to provision required master and slave nodes for the cluster. The next stage is **BOOTSTRAPPING**, where user-defined actions are run on the cluster including any required customizations or installation of software/packages/tools. After successful completion of the **BOOSTRAPPING** state, the cluster will be in a **RUNNING** state to execute the Job Flow with required Job Steps.

When a cluster terminates after successful completion of all Job Steps in a transient cluster, it enters the **SHUTTING_DOWN** state to delete the data in HDFS and stop servers. After successful shutdown, the cluster status changes to **COMPLETED**. However, if **termination protection** is not enabled on the cluster, then any problem or error encountered during cluster process will terminate the associated servers and delete the data in HDFS with a cluster status of **FAILED**. When the user initiates termination of the cluster, it first enters the **SHUTTING_DOWN** state and then on successful termination, the status is changes to **TERMINATED**.

Keep alive

When launching an EMR cluster, you can specify whether it should be long running or transient based on the needs. If you configure the EMR cluster to be long running, then it will be in the **WAITING** state after successful completion or failure of Job Steps. However, a transient EMR cluster will automatically terminate after successful completion or failure of Job Steps.

Termination protection

This is one of the new features added by EMR. Enabling **termination protection** on your EMR clusters lets you ensure that the nodes aren't terminated accidently from the AWS console, by any API call, or by any CLI tool. You can use this feature when you do not want to lose data present on your nodes, even accidently.

By default, **termination protection** is disabled for an EMR cluster. When **termination protection** is enabled, you must explicitly remove the **termination protection** setting from the AWS management console before you can terminate the cluster.

The **keep alive** and **termination protection** features are similar, but the protections they provide are different. The **keep alive** feature ensures that a cluster is kept running even after all the added job steps are completed, but the cluster can be terminated via `TerminateJobFlow` API call or on errors. With **keep alive** disabled, **termination protection** lets the cluster terminate on successful completion of all steps, but it does not allow the cluster to be terminated in case of any user action, errors, or the `TerminateJobFlow` API call.

The following diagram illustrates the EMR cluster's life cycle:

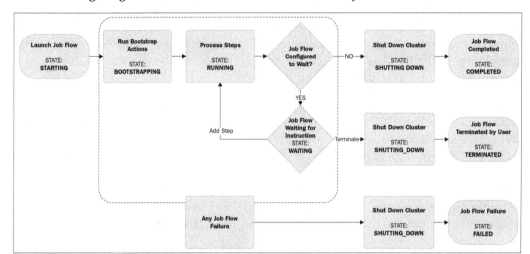

Hadoop filesystem on EMR – S3 and HDFS

EMR supports using AWS S3 or HDFS as filesystems for the hosted Hadoop. We can use S3 for input data to jobs and output data of the EMR cluster or mix it with HDFS usage. However, if we use S3 to store the input data, then we can run multiple clusters that are performing different jobs on the same dataset.

We can load the input data to jobs from S3 into HDFS for job execution and then load the output data from HDFS into S3 for persistence if we terminate a cluster. Amazon provides a toolkit to read or write data from HDFS to S3. It will be very useful to transfer data when you want to migrate an existing cluster from the data center to AWS.

> If you have uploaded files to Amazon S3, they are stored using the S3 native filesystem (S3N). Earlier, it was required to have s3n:// in file paths instead of s3:// for all files that you upload. Now on Amazon EMR, both s3n:// and s3:// map to the S3 native filesystem.

EMR use cases

Amazon EMR can be used to build a variety of applications such as recommendation engines, data analysis, log processing, event/clickstream analysis, data transformations (ETL), fraud detection, scientific simulations, genomics, financial analysis, or data correlation in various industries. The following section outlines some of the use cases in detail.

Web log processing

We can use EMR to process logs to understand the usage of content such as video, file downloads, top web URLs accessed by end users, user consumption from different parts of the world, and many more. We can process any web or mobile application logs using EMR to understand specific business insights relevant for your business. We can move all our web access application or mobile logs to Amazon S3 for analysis using EMR even if we are not using AWS for running our production applications.

Clickstream analysis

By using clickstream analysis, we can segment users into different groups and understand their behaviors with respect to advertisements or application usage. Ad networks or advertisers can perform clickstream analysis on ad-impression logs to deliver more effective campaigns or advertisements to end users. Reports generated from this analysis can include various metrics such as source traffic distribution, purchase funnel, lead source ROI, and abandoned carts among others.

Product recommendation engine

Recommendation engines can be built using EMR for e-commerce, retail, or web businesses. Many of the e-commerce businesses have a large inventory of products across different categories while regularly adding new products or categories. It will be very difficult for end users to search and identify the products quickly. With recommendation engines, we can help end users to quickly find relevant products or suggest products based on what they are viewing and so on. We may also want to notify users via an e-mail based on their past purchase behavior.

Scientific simulations

When you need distributed processing with large-scale infrastructure for scientific or research simulations, EMR can be of great help. We can quickly launch large clusters in a matter of minutes and install specific MapReduce programs for analysis using EMR. AWS also offers genomics datasets for free on S3.

Data transformations

We can perform complex **extract, transform, and load** (ETL) processes using EMR for either data analysis or data warehousing needs. It can be as simple as transforming XML file data into JSON data for further usage or moving all financial transaction records of a bank into a common date-time format for archiving purposes. You can also use EMR to move data between different systems in AWS such as DynamoDB, Redshift, S3, and many more.

Summary

In this chapter, we learned about the Amazon EMR along with its features and architecture. We understood the concepts related to EMR for various node types, tasks, Job Flows, and Job Steps in detail. We discussed all the states of an EMR. We also learned the various ways we can program our Big Data solutions on EMR.

In the next chapter, we will create our `hello world` solution using Hadoop (custom JAR) and will get ready to launch a cluster on EMR.

5
Programming Hadoop on Amazon EMR

We will now create a solution to the problem we discussed in *Chapter 2, MapReduce*, using Hadoop 2.2.0. We will create the solution in Java, and by the end of this chapter, you will have created a JAR with a solution and will have tested it locally on a sample input data.

Hello World in Hadoop

Let's quickly recap the problem we discussed in *Chapter 2, MapReduce*.

Problem statement

Given access logs, you need to count the number of hits to your website per country. The input access logs will be in the following form:

```
Date, Requesting-IP-Address(remote host)
```

We are going to create a solution for this problem in Java to be executed over Hadoop 2.2.0. In *Chapter 9, Hadoop Streaming and Advanced Hadoop Customizations*, we will see how we can use Hadoop streaming to create mapper and reducer even in other languages such as Python and Ruby among others.

Development Environment Setup

We will use Hadoop 2.2.0. It requires Java 7 or later versions of Java 6 (Oracle 1.6.0_31). It is recommended that you use Java 7 (preferably Oracle Java). You can refer to `http://wiki.apache.org/hadoop/HadoopJavaVersions` for more information on available JREs for Hadoop.

We like to use Eclipse as our preferred IDE, you may use any other IDE as per your choice. We also recommend you to use some flavor of Unix as the OS. We are using Ubuntu.

Now, let's have a look at the step-by-step checklist for you to be ready to create your first Hadoop MapReduce solution. We will assume the use of Eclipse as IDE.

Step 1 – Installing the Eclipse IDE

Confirm that you have one of the latest versions of either Eclipse IDE for Java Developers or Eclipse Standard installed along with Java 7. You may follow the instructions to install them from their official pages. You can get Eclipse from their official download page at `https://www.eclipse.org/downloads/`.

Step 2 – Downloading Hadoop 2.2.0

The following substeps can be used to download Hadoop 2.2.0 distribution:

1. Go to the **Apache Download Mirrors** page for Apache Hadoop: `http://www.apache.org/dyn/closer.cgi/hadoop/common/`.

2. After selecting your nearest mirror, you will be taken to a page which should have a listing of Hadoop releases available for download.

3. Click on **hadoop-2.2.0** from the listing.

4. Download `hadoop-2.2.0.tar.gz`.

Step 3 – Unzipping Hadoop Distribution

Unzip the downloaded `tar.gz` file, say to `/<hadoop-2.2.0-base-path>`.

> We will not be setting up a single node cluster; if you want to set it up, you can follow the instructions provided at `http://hadoop.apache.org/docs/r2.2.0/hadoop-project-dist/hadoop-common/SingleCluster.html`.

Step 4 – Creating a new Java project in Eclipse

Start Eclipse and create a new Java project. Let's name it `HadoopHelloWorld` as shown in the following screenshot:

Step 5 – Adding dependencies to the project

Add the following two JARs to your build path:

- `hadoop-common-2.2.0.jar`: This can be found in the unzipped directory at `/<hadoop-2.2.0-base-path>/share/hadoop/common/`

- `hadoop-mapreduce-client-core-2.2.0.jar`: This can be found in the unzipped directory at `/<hadoop-2.2.0-base-path>/share/hadoop/mapreduce/`

As you can see, Hadoop now has most of its components available as separate modules, so you only use what you need. The two libraries mentioned are required to compile our code and it has most of the classes and utilities we need to create the MapReduce solution for our problem.

In order to add these external JARs to the build path in Hadoop, you have to perform the following steps:

1. Add a folder named `lib` to the project created in *Step 4 – Creating a new Java project in Eclipse*.

2. Copy the mentioned JARs in this folder.

3. Right-click on the project name in **Package Explorer**.

4. Select **Build Path** and then **Configure Build Path**.

5. Click on **Add Jars**, select our project **HadoopHelloWorld** and add these two JARs from the `lib` folder.

After addition, your **Java Build Path** window should look like the following:

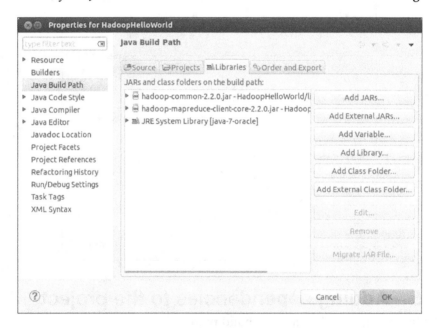

We are now ready to code.

Let's first create the following two packages which will host our classes:

- `learning.bigdata.main`: This will have our driver class
- `learning.bigdata.mapreduce`: This will have our mapper and reduce implementations

At this stage, your **Package Explorer** window should look like the following:

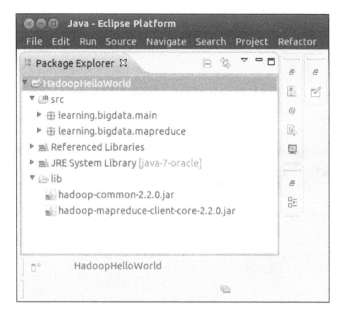

We will create the following three classes as part of our solution:

- `learning.bigdata.mapreduce.HitsByCountryMapper`: This will be our mapper implementation that extends `org.apache.hadoop.mapreduce.Mapper`

- `learning.bigdata.mapreduce.HitsByCountryReducer`: This will be our reducer implementation that extends `org.apache.hadoop.mapreduce.Reducer`

- `learning.bigdata.main.HitsByCountry`: This will be the driver class that extends `org.apache.hadoop.conf.Configured` and implements `org.apache.hadoop.util.Tool`

Mapper implementation

As discussed in *Chapter 2, MapReduce*, our mapper is going to process each line in the input (simplified access log), find the country to which the IP address belongs, and emit the key-value pair in the form of `<Country, 1>`.

Apache Hadoop provides a basic mapper implementation present in the form of an `org.apache.hadoop.mapreduce.Mapper` class.

You just need to extend this class and override the required methods.

The `org.apache.hadoop.mapreduce.Mapper` class has the following methods:

- `setup`
- `map`
- `cleanup`
- `run`

Setup

By default, this method is empty and is called once per map task at the beginning before processing the input split. It should be overridden if any statement or set of statements are required to be executed at the beginning of each map task.

It is defined in the `Mapper` class as follows:

```
protected void setup(Context context) throws IOException,
  InterruptedException {
    // This method is empty
  }
```

Map

In a default implementation, this method is called once for each key-value pair in the input split. Most often, you will just be overriding the `map` function and provide the custom implementation required, but the default is the `identity` function.

It is defined in the `Mapper` class as follows:

```
protected void map(KEYIN key, VALUEIN value,
                   Context context) throws IOException,
                     InterruptedException {
    context.write((KEYOUT) key, (VALUEOUT) value);
  }
```

Cleanup

By default, this method is empty and is called once per map task at the end after processing the input split and should be overridden if any statement or set of statements are to be executed at the end of each map task.

It is defined in the `Mapper` class as follows:

```
protected void cleanup(Context context) throws IOException,
  InterruptedException {
    // This method is empty
  }
```

Run

This is the actual method which is run internally. This method defines the order in which the mentioned three methods are executed, so unless you absolutely know what you are doing, you should not override this method in your mapper implementations.

Overriding this method provides you complete control over execution of the mapper.

It is defined in the `Mapper` class as follows:

```
public void run(Context context) throws IOException,
  InterruptedException {
    setup(context);
    try {
      while (context.nextKeyValue()) {
        map(context.getCurrentKey(), context.getCurrentValue(),
          context);
      }
    } finally {
      cleanup(context);
    }
}
```

We are going to override only the `map` function for our solution. Let's create a class named `HitsByCountryMapper` in the `learning.bigdata.mapreduce` package. Its signature will be as follows:

```
public class HitsByCountryMapper extends Mapper<LongWritable,
  Text, Text, IntWritable> {
// map function implementation here along with any other utility
  methods
}
```

You may have noticed the four sets of `Writable` types mentioned as part of the signature extending the `Mapper` class. The following displays how the `Mapper` class signature looks:

```
public class Mapper<KEYIN, VALUEIN, KEYOUT, VALUEOUT> {
...
}
```

In our case, the input key is expected to be read into `LongWritable` and input value is expected to be read into `Text`. The choice of these two data types depends on what input format you are using, as the input format will read the data from the input split and pass it on to the `map` method. In our case, we are going to use `TextInputFormat` that generates keys of type `LongWritable` and values of type `Text`.

The mapper output key-value pair also needs its types to be defined. There also needs to be an agreement over the types between mapper and reducer. That is, the output key-value types of the mapper should match the input key-value pair of the reducer. Also, these need to be defined in the driver class while creating the job. We will see how this is done in the *Driver implementation* section.

In our case, since we want to emit a string (`country name`) and a count (value 1) as our key and value respectively from our mapper, we have the mapper output key-value types as `Text` and `IntWritable`.

Hence, combining all four in place of the following placeholders, we get the following code:

```
<KEYIN, VALUEIN, KEYOUT, VALUEOUT>
```

We have the following writable types:

```
<LongWritable, Text, Text, IntWritable>
```

Create two properties within `HitsByCountryMapper`, which will hold the key and value to be emitted by our `map` method. You just set the appropriate value to these properties and emit them. This can be done as follows:

```
private Text outputKey = new Text();
private IntWritable outputValue = new IntWritable();
```

Let's now create our `map` method implementation. The signature of our `map` method will be as follows:

```
@Override
public void map(LongWritable key, Text value, Context context)
  throws IOException, InterruptedException {
// process each access log line here
}
```

You can see that the method parameters' types need to correspond to the mapper input key and value types, that is, `LongWritable` and `Text` respectively.

`TextInputFormat` uses either linefeed or carriage-return to signal the end of a line and reads the position in the file as `key`, and the line of text is read as `value`.

Hence, your single line of access log will come as `value` to the `map` method. You will need to get the IP address from the input value and you can ignore the input key. The value is expected to be in the following format:

```
Date, IP-Address
```

You can get the IP address simply by splitting the value, as shown in the following code:

```
String valueString = value.toString();
String[] row = valueString.split(","); // Split the value string
  to get Date and ipAddress
String ipAddress = row[1]; // row[0]= Date and row[1]=ipAddress
```

Now, you need to get the country name to which this IP address belongs. Ideally, we would use a commonly available database such as `Geoip`, which also provides Java-based APIs to connect to its database file having IP to country mapping. In the `setup` method, we can create the database reader and use that inside our `map` method to convert an IP address to its corresponding country name. We will see such implementation in *Chapter 10, Use Case – Analyzing CloudFront Logs Using Amazon EMR*.

For now, we will create a method that will emit fake country names, but will do that consistently. So, you can create a simple implementation named `getCountryNameFromIpAddress`, which would take the IP address as a parameter and return a country name, as shown in the following code:

```
private final static String[] COUNTRIES = { "India", "UK", "US",
  "China" };
private static String getCountryNameFromIpAddress(String
  ipAddress) {
  if (ipAddress != null && !ipAddress.isEmpty()) {
    int randomIndex = Math.abs(ipAddress.hashCode()) %
      COUNTRIES.length;
    return COUNTRIES[randomIndex];
  }
  return null;
}
```

You can now use this method in the map method to get the country name. This can be done as follows:

```
String countryName = getCountryNameFromIpAddress(ipAddress);
```

At last, you will just set the outputKey and outputValue properties and write them into the context variable, which is passed on to the map method along with the input key and value, as follows:

```
outputKey.set(countryName);
outputValue.set(1);
context.write(outputKey, outputValue);
```

Finally, we have the complete mapper implementation as follows:

```
public class HitsByCountryMapper extends Mapper<LongWritable,
    Text, Text, IntWritable> {

    private final static String[] COUNTRIES = { "India", "UK", "US",
        "China" };
    private Text outputKey = new Text();
    private IntWritable outputValue = new IntWritable();

    @Override
    public void map(LongWritable key, Text value, Context context)
        throws IOException, InterruptedException {

        // 'value' is expected to have one line from input file
        // It is expected to be in the following format:
        // Date, ipAddress
        try {
            String valueString = value.toString();

            // Split the value string to get Date and ipAddress
            String[] row = valueString.split(",");

            // row[0]= Date and row[1]=ipAddress
            String ipAddress = row[1];

            // Get the country name to which the ipAddress belongs
            String countryName = getCountryNameFromIpAddress(ipAddress);
            outputKey.set(countryName);
            outputValue.set(1);
            context.write(outputKey, outputValue);

        } catch (ArrayIndexOutOfBoundsException ex) {
            context.getCounter("Custom counters",
                "MAPPER_EXCEPTION_COUNTER").increment(1);
```

```
      ex.printStackTrace();
    }
  }

  /**
   * This method is just for testing purposes and does not return
     the correct country for a given IP Address.
   * It just returns one of the countries from { "India", "UK",
     "US", "China" }, on the basis of ipAddress.hashCode()
   *
   * @param ipAddress
   * @return The country name.
   */
  private static String getCountryNameFromIpAddress(String
    ipAddress) {

    if (ipAddress != null && !ipAddress.isEmpty()) {
      int randomIndex = Math.abs(ipAddress.hashCode()) %
        COUNTRIES.length;
      return COUNTRIES[randomIndex];
    }
    return null;
  }
}
```

You may have seen one additional detail in there at the end of the map method, that is, you can have a global counter that Hadoop helps to aggregate across all map and reduce tasks. In our case, we are creating our custom counter named MAPPER_EXCEPTION_COUNTER and it is incremented when an ArrayIndexOutOfBoundsException is caught. This can happen when we have a corrupted access log line in our input. Having such a global counter may help us know how many corrupt lines were present in our input data and decide accordingly whether it is within a tolerable limit or whether some appropriate action needs to be undertaken.

You can get an instance of a Counter object from the context object. The getCounter method, which we are using here takes in two parameters: a counter group name and the counter name.

Using the increment method of the Counter class, you can increment the counter accordingly. In our case, within the catch block, we have the following statement incrementing the counter:

```
context.getCounter("Custom counters",
  "MAPPER_EXCEPTION_COUNTER").increment(1);
```

Let's now move on to our reducer implementation.

Reducer implementation

As discussed in *Chapter 2, MapReduce*, our reducer is going to receive input in the form of `<Country, [1,1,1,1,...,1]>` and it will sum the values, which will represent the number of hits from that country.

Apache Hadoop provides a basic reducer implementation present in the form of an `org.apache.hadoop.mapreduce.Reducer` class.

You just need to extend this class and override the required methods.

The `org.apache.hadoop.mapreduce.Reducer` class also has methods similar to that of the `Mapper` class and instead of the `map` method, there is a `reduce` method. The `setup` and `cleanup` methods serve the same purpose as they do in the `Mapper` class.

Let's see the `reduce` and `run` methods as present in the `Reducer` class.

Reduce

In default implementation, this method is called once for each unique key emitted from the mapper. Most often, you will just be overriding the `reduce` function and providing the custom implementation as required, but the default is the `identity` function.

It is defined in the `Reducer` class as follows:

```
protected void reduce(KEYIN key, Iterable<VALUEIN> values,
  Context context
                      ) throws IOException, InterruptedException
                      {
    for(VALUEIN value: values) {
      context.write((KEYOUT) key, (VALUEOUT) value);
    }
  }
```

Run

Same as it is in the `Mapper` class, this is the actual method which runs internally. This can be overridden in order to control how a reduce task works. But precautions should be taken while overriding this method and it should not be overridden unless you know exactly what you are doing.

It is defined in the `Reducer` class as follows:

```
public void run(Context context) throws IOException,
  InterruptedException {
    setup(context);
    try {
      while (context.nextKey()) {
        reduce(context.getCurrentKey(), context.getValues(),
          context);
        // If a back up store is used, reset it
        Iterator<VALUEIN> iter = context.getValues().iterator();
        if(iter instanceof ReduceContext.ValueIterator) {
          ((ReduceContext.ValueIterator<VALUEIN>)iter).
resetBackupStore();
        }
      }
    } finally {
      cleanup(context);
    }
  }
```

We are going to override only the `reduce` function for our solution.

Let's create a class named `HitsByCountryReducer` in the `learning.bigdata.mapreduce` package.

Its signature will be as follows:

```
public class HitsByCountryReducer extends Reducer<Text,
  IntWritable, Text, IntWritable> {
// reduce function implementation here
}
```

As you can see, the input key-value pair types is consistent with the mapper output key-value pair types. The reducer output key-value pair types are `Text` and `IntWritable` for key and value respectively. Our output will have the key as the country name, a string; hence, we have `Text` as our output key type. The value we will have is going to be a sum; hence, `IntWritable`. If you expect your hits count to be large enough not to be accommodated as an integer, you may use other types such as `LongWritable` in place of `IntWritable`.

First, in the `Reducer` class, let's declare the required `outputKey` and `outputValue` along with a variable that will hold the sum count. This part will be as follows:

```
private Text outputKey = new Text();
private IntWritable outputValue = new IntWritable();
private int count = 0;
```

Let's now create our `reduce` method implementation. The signature of our `reduce` method will be as follows:

```
@Override
protected void reduce(Text key, Iterable<IntWritable> values,
  Context context) throws IOException,
     InterruptedException {
// process each unique key emitted from Mapper, basically, process
  every country name
}
```

You can see that the types of method parameters need to correspond to the mapper's output key and value types, that is, `Text` and `IntWritable` respectively. The `reduce` method receives a key and an `Iterable` object to iterate over the list of values. It also receives a `context` object.

The task we need to perform in the `reduce` method is very simple; we just need to find the sum of all the occurrences of a country name. This can be done as follows within the `reduce` method:

```
count=0;
Iterator<IntWritable> iterator = values.iterator();
while (iterator.hasNext()) {
  IntWritable value = iterator.next();
  count += value.get();
}
```

The `count` variable is reinitialized to `0` so that the count might not be carried to the processing of the next key, that is, the next country name.

Now, you just need to set the output key to be the same as what has been received by the `reduce` method, that is, the country name. The output value will be the count. This can be done as follows:

```
outputKey.set(key);
outputValue.set(count);
context.write(outputKey, outputValue);
```

The following is how your complete reducer implementation should look:

```
public class HitsByCountryReducer extends Reducer<Text,
  IntWritable, Text, IntWritable> {

  private Text outputKey = new Text();
  private IntWritable outputValue = new IntWritable();
  private int count = 0;
```

```
protected void reduce(Text key, Iterable<IntWritable> values,
    Context context) throws IOException,
        InterruptedException {

    count = 0;
    Iterator<IntWritable> iterator = values.iterator();
    while (iterator.hasNext()) {
        IntWritable value = iterator.next();
        count += value.get();
    }
    outputKey.set(key);
    outputValue.set(count);
    context.write(outputKey, outputValue);
    }
}
```

Driver implementation

The driver class is the one which has the main method and provides the place where the Hadoop job is created and its mapper and reducer along with a bunch of other configurations and settings are declared. The job is initiated from here itself.

We will name this class HitsByCountry and let's create this class inside the learning.bigdata.main package. Your driver class should have the following signature:

```
public class HitsByCountry extends Configured implements Tool {
    // Here we will have the main method as well as the
    overridden implementation of run method
}
```

The driver class extends the Configured class and implements the Tool interface. There are many Hadoop configurations you can set in the driver class while creating a job. For example, you can set the number of reducers using the mapred.reduce.tasks configuration and you can set the separator between the key and value you will have in your reducer output while using TextOutputFormat with mapred.textoutputformat.separator as the configuration name, and so on. Inside your driver class, you can create an object of the org.apache.hadoop.conf.Configuration class and set a particular Hadoop configuration in the following fashion:

```
Configuration conf = new Configuration();
conf.set("mapred.textoutputformat.separator", ",");
```

Also, what if you need to change this configuration on the fly, that is, after the JAR has been created, or what if you need to test various values of the same configuration parameter? If you are going to have the configuration parameters set explicitly inside the driver class, each time you will need to change the value, recompile it, and build a new JAR. That's just painful and a waste of time.

By extending the `Configured` class along with implementing the `Tool` interface, we get the liberty to use the `Configured` class's `setConf()` method and pass these Hadoop configurations via command line while executing our jobs. These configurations can be provided as command-line arguments along with -D. For example, it can be as follows:

```
-D mapred.reduce.tasks=2 <comma separated input paths>
<output path>
```

It should be noted that these command-line arguments should be placed at the beginning, followed by actual job arguments. It internally uses `GenericOptionsParser` to separate out the Hadoop configuration parameters from other actual job parameters such as the input and output paths.

We will use the ToolRunner's static method, `run`, to launch our job. This method expects an implementation of the `Tool` interface, which our driver class itself is and a `String` array of arguments. Now it's the responsibility of this class to segregate the actual job parameters and Hadoop configurations along with other generic options such as `-libjars` and `-files` among others. This means that the args variable in our `main` method will receive all the command-line parameters but the args variable in our overridden `run` method will only receive the actual job parameters as if only these were provided to the job. If you are confused, it will all become clear in a while, let's have a look at how our `main` method should look:

```
public static void main(String[] args) throws Exception {
  if (args.length < 2) {
    System.out.println("Usage: HitsByCountry <comma separated
      input directories> <output dir>");
    System.exit(-1);
  }
  int result = ToolRunner.run(new HitsByCountry(), args);
  System.exit(result);
}
```

As you can see, the code in our `main` method is straightforward and minimal, thanks to `Tool` and `Configured`. In the first few lines, we have just made sure that a minimal number of arguments are received by the application, that is, one comma separated list of input paths and one path to the output directory.

> At this point, it would be prudent to mention that Hadoop expects that the output path you are going to mention does not exist; otherwise, it would complain that the file already exists.

Now, let's see how our `run` method will be implemented. Its signature is as follows:

```
@Override
public int run(String[] args) throws Exception {
// Here you will have code to create a job, launch it and wait for
  its completion
}
```

First, inside the `run` method, you will get an object of the `Configuration` class using the `getConf()` method of the `Configured` class that our driver is extending from. Also, using that object of `Configuration`, you can get the instance of the `Job` class, as shown in the following code:

```
Configuration conf = getConf();
Job job = Job.getInstance(conf);
```

> Since Hadoop Version 2, using the constructor of the `Job` class has been deprecated, and instead you should use the `getInstance(Configuration conf)` factory method to get an instance of the `Job` class.

Next, you need to set the job name by which your job can be identified:

```
job.setJobName("Calculating hits by country");
```

The next thing you need to do is specify a class name, using which the Hadoop job can decide which JAR should be passed on to the worker nodes in order to perform the map and reduce tasks. Basically, you need to provide a class that will identify the JAR in which the mapper and reducer implementations are present. This is required as your implementation might have more than one JAR in its class path. It is also possible that your driver class might reside in a different JAR than that of your mapper and reducer implementations. Also, you should at least make sure that both the mapper and reducer implementations are present in the same JAR. In our case, all of our implementations including our driver class are going to be a part of the same JAR; hence, we can use our driver class itself, as follows:

```
job.setJarByClass(HitsByCountry.class);
```

Next, you will need to declare your mapper and reducer implementations to take up the job. You will also need to provide the output key class and output value class for both mapper and reducer implementations.

In our case, these steps can be done by using the following set of statements:

```
job.setMapperClass(HitsByCountryMapper.class);
job.setMapOutputKeyClass(Text.class);
job.setMapOutputValueClass(IntWritable.class);

job.setReducerClass(HitsByCountryReducer.class);
job.setOutputKeyClass(Text.class);
job.setOutputValueClass(IntWritable.class);
```

> You will notice that we need not provide the input key and value classes for either mapper or reducer. The input types for the mapper are decided by the input format you will use, while the input types for the reducer are determined by the output types of mapper.

Now, you will set the input and output formats for the job. We will use `TextInputFormat` and `TextOutputFormat` respectively. Hadoop does provide many other predefined input and output formats, and you can even override the base classes and create custom formats, as follows:

```
job.setInputFormatClass(TextInputFormat.class);
job.setOutputFormatClass(TextOutputFormat.class);
```

We are almost done. You just need to add the input paths and the output path as received via the command-line arguments.

As explained earlier, even if the command-line arguments submitted while executing the job have generic options having Hadoop configurations among others, the actual job parameters that are passed after the generic options will be received by the `run` method in the original order.

Consider that your job was executed as follows:

```
$hadoop jar hits-by-country.jar -D
mapred.textoutputformat.separator=,
/home/awesome-hadoop/input/file1.csv home/awesome-hadoop/output/
```

Your `main` method would receive all the arguments and the configuration to set the `TextOutputFormat` separator to be a comma instead of the default tab, but your `run` method will only receive the following:

```
/home/awesome-hadoop/input/file1.csv home/awesome-hadoop/output/
```

Hence, `args[0]` will have the input path(s) and `args[1]` will have the output path. You can set the input paths and the output path as follows:

```
FileInputFormat.setInputPaths(job, args[0]);
FileOutputFormat.setOutputPath(job, new Path(args[1]));
```

One last thing you need to do now is to launch the job and wait for its completion. We will use the `job` object's `waitForCompletion()` method to do just that:

```
boolean success = job.waitForCompletion(true);
```

The full implementation of your driver class will look as follows:

```
public class HitsByCountry extends Configured implements Tool {

  private static final String JOB_NAME = "Calculating hits by
    country";

  public static void main(String[] args) throws Exception {

    if (args.length < 2) {
      System.out.println("Usage: HitsByCountry <comma separated
        input directories> <output dir>");
      System.exit(-1);
    }

    int result = ToolRunner.run(new HitsByCountry(), args);
    System.exit(result);
  }

  @Override
  public int run(String[] args) throws Exception {
    Configuration conf = getConf();
    Job job = Job.getInstance(conf);

    job.setJarByClass(HitsByCountry.class);
    job.setJobName(JOB_NAME);

    job.setMapperClass(HitsByCountryMapper.class);
    job.setMapOutputKeyClass(Text.class);
    job.setMapOutputValueClass(IntWritable.class);
    job.setReducerClass(HitsByCountryReducer.class);
    job.setOutputKeyClass(Text.class);
    job.setOutputValueClass(IntWritable.class);
```

```
job.setInputFormatClass(TextInputFormat.class);
job.setOutputFormatClass(TextOutputFormat.class);

FileInputFormat.setInputPaths(job, args[0]);
FileOutputFormat.setOutputPath(job, new Path(args[1]));

boolean success = job.waitForCompletion(true);
return success ? 0 : 1;
    }
}
```

That's all. You are done creating your *Hello World* in Hadoop. We will now create the JAR and test it locally once before we go ahead and launch an EMR cluster and execute this solution here.

Building a JAR

Now, you need to create the runnable JAR to be provided to Hadoop. There are other ways to create a JAR; however, since we are using Eclipse, we will export a JAR from here itself.

Follow these steps to export a JAR:

1. In the **Package Explorer** window, right-click on the project name (**HadoopHelloWorld**) and click on **Export**.

2. Select **Java** and then **JAR file** from the list and click on **Next**.

3. Provide the path you want your JAR to be created at, which will also include the JAR name. You may name it `hits-by-country.jar`. Leave other options in their default state and click on **Next**.

4. Leave the default option on the **JAR packaging options** section and click on **Next**.

5. In the **JAR Manifest Specification** section, in the bottom, specify the **Main** class.

6. Click on **Browse** and select our driver class (**HitsByCountry**) from the list. Click on **OK** and then click on **Finish**.

7. That's all, your JAR should be exported successfully. Let's assume that you have exported your JAR in the following path: `/<test-base-path>/bin/hits-by-country.jar`.

Executing the solution locally

Now, let's try to execute this solution locally. You should ensure that the JAVA_HOME environment variable has been properly set.

We already have a JAR ready with us, what we need is a sample input file to run our local test over; you can create a sample input file with random dates and random IP addresses in the following form:

```
2014-05-01,180.166.24.11
2014-05-02,113.57.188.101
...
2014-05-06,183.22.251.177
2014-05-06,180.166.24.11
2014-05-07,180.166.24.11
2014-05-07,223.87.29.14
```

Let's assume that you have created this file at the following path:

```
/<test-base-path>/input/sample.csv
```

In order to test the correctness of your MapReduce code, you need not set up a local cluster, you can run hadoop as any other command/script. In order to do that, let's first go to the location where we had downloaded and unzipped the hadoop-2.2.0 distribution in an earlier section.

Make sure that JAVA_HOME is set appropriately, or alternatively, open <hadoop-2.2.0-base-path>/etc/hadoop/hadoop-env.sh.

You will see the following line in here:

```
export JAVA_HOME=${JAVA_HOME}
```

You can edit this line to have the required path as follows:

```
export JAVA_HOME=/usr/lib/jvm/java-7-oracle/
```

Now, let's move to the directory where we have the hadoop executable:

```
$ cd /<hadoop-2.2.0-base-path>/bin
```

Execute our JAR with the following command, making sure that the output folder doesn't already exist:

```
$ hadoop jar /<test-base-path>/bin/hits-by-country.jar -D
mapred.textoutputformat.separator=,
/<test-base-path>/input/sample.csv /<test-base-path>/output/try1/
```

Your job should execute successfully and at the end, it should have something similar to that shown in the following command:

```
14/06/10 04:34:46 INFO mapreduce.Job:  map 100% reduce 100%
14/06/10 04:34:46 INFO mapreduce.Job: Job job_local1362926395_0001
completed successfully
14/06/10 04:34:46 INFO mapreduce.Job: Counters: 27
    File System Counters
      FILE: Number of bytes read=7901699
      FILE: Number of bytes written=8202415
      FILE: Number of read operations=0
      FILE: Number of large read operations=0
      FILE: Number of write operations=0
    Map-Reduce Framework
      Map input records=3526
      Map output records=3526
      Map output bytes=30565
      Map output materialized bytes=37623
      Input split bytes=134
      Combine input records=0
      Combine output records=0
      Reduce input groups=4
      Reduce shuffle bytes=0
      Reduce input records=3526
      Reduce output records=4
      Spilled Records=7052
      Shuffled Maps =0
      Failed Shuffles=0
      Merged Map outputs=0
      GC time elapsed (ms)=5
      CPU time spent (ms)=0
      Physical memory (bytes) snapshot=0
      Virtual memory (bytes) snapshot=0
      Total committed heap usage (bytes)=384696320
    File Input Format Counters
      Bytes Read=90244
    File Output Format Counters
      Bytes Written=47
```

Verifying the output

On a successful execution, you should have the output files created in the `output` directory you had mentioned as an argument while executing:

```
$ ls /<test-base-path>/output/try1/
part-r-00000   _SUCCESS
```

You can see that there is a file named `part-r-00000`; this is the naming convention followed by Hadoop wherein each reducer writes an output file. So if we had two reducers, we will get two output files, namely, `part-r-00000` and `part-r-00001`.

Now, let's check out what output we have got:

```
$ cat /<test-base-path>/output/try1/part-r-00000
China,819
India,1142
UK,633
US,932
```

There you go, you have a number of hits per country in your output. Also, since we had used a dummy method that emits only one of the four country names, we have all of them in the preceding output. You might get some other hit counts value per country, depending on your sample input data and your implementation of `getCountryNameFromIpAddress(ipAddress)`.

Summary

We created a solution to a very simple counting problem and we aptly called it `Hello World in Hadoop`. We went through all the components you would have in a Hadoop MapReduce implementation in Java.

Now, we are all set to launch a cluster on EMR and test this simple solution that we created. In our next chapter, we will start with the creation of a S3 bucket and uploading the solution `.jar` file as well as the sample input file, and then follow it by launching an EMR cluster, which would execute our solution. On its completion, we will download the output and check it out. We will also learn the various Hadoop job models available on EMR.

6

Executing Hadoop Jobs on an Amazon EMR Cluster

In this chapter, we will now see how to launch an EMR cluster via the AWS management console. We will then execute the solution that we created in the previous chapter in this cluster. Out of various ways to program a solution on EMR, as we saw in *Chapter 4*, *Amazon EMR – Hadoop on Amazon Web Services*, we chose the custom JAR technique, and we will use the JAR we created in the previous chapter.

Before you go ahead and launch your EMR cluster, you will need to make sure that the following two things are taken care of:

- You need to have an EC2 key pair. If you do not have it, you can get it generated from your AWS management console. You will need this to SSH into the master node of the EMR cluster.

- You need to upload the input files and the custom JAR we created in *Chapter 4*, *Amazon EMR – Hadoop on Amazon Web Services*, to Amazon S3. EMR will fetch the input as well as the program to be executed (a JAR file) by the cluster from S3.

Creating an EC2 key pair

If you already have an EC2 key pair that you have generated while launching an EC2 machine, you can use this while launching the EMR cluster. Also, if you do not have it, you need not worry as you can generate it with a few clicks on the AWS management console.

Perform the following steps to generate an EC2 key value pair:

1. Log in to your AWS management console and go to the EC2 Dashboard by navigating to **Services | All AWS Services | EC2**. Also from the top-right corner, select the region for which you want this EC2 key pair to be generated.

2. From the left-hand side navigation pane, click on **Key Pairs**; you can find this in the **NETWORK & SECURITY** section.

3. Click on **Create Key Pair**; you will have a pop up as follows:

4. You should key in an appropriate name for the key pair, and click on **Create**. This will create the key pair and the private key file will be automatically downloaded by the browser. It will be a PEM file for you to use while connecting to the EC2 machines or EMR clusters created with this key pair. The filename will have the base name the same as the key pair name you gave it in the previous step and the extension will be .pem. For example, if you have created the key pair with the name learning_bigdata_emr, the filename would be learning_bigdata_emr.pem.

> Amazon uses public key cryptography, which uses a public key to encrypt data, and the recipient uses a private key to decrypt the data. This set of public and private keys are called a key pair. The .pem file is the private key. You should store this .pem file in a safe location because if you lose it, there is no way for you to get this same key pair generated again. AWS doesn't store this private key.

5. If you are using an SSH client on Linux/Mac to connect to your master node, you will need to provide the appropriate permission to the `.pem` file restricting the permissions so that only you can read it. Considering that your key pair file name is `learning_bigdata_emr.pem`, this can be done by the following command:

```
$ chmod 400 learning_bigdata_emr.pem
```

Your key pair is now ready to be used to launch an EC2 machine or the EMR cluster.

Creating a S3 bucket for input data and JAR

You will need to create an Amazon S3 bucket to hold the following four things:

- Input file(s)
- The custom JAR executable
- Output file(s)
- Hadoop job's logfiles generated by the EMR cluster

Perform the following steps to create a S3 bucket and upload the custom JAR we have created, and also upload the sample input file on which we have executed this locally in the previous chapter:

1. Log in to your AWS management console and go to the EC2 Dashboard by navigating to **Services** | **All AWS Services** | **S3**. S3 doesn't require region selection.

2. Click on **Create Bucket** and provide a suitable name for the bucket. Let's say you named your bucket `learning-bigdata`. It is to be kept in mind that S3 bucket names are unique globally, so your bucket name will be allowed only if no other bucket exists with the same name.

   At this point, your browser screen will look as follows:

3. Create an appropriate folder structure inside the bucket. Click on **Create Folder** and create a folder named `HadoopHelloWorld`. Now, click on the newly created folder name and within that folder create three more folders; one each for input files, binaries (JAR), and output files. You can also create the folder for EMR logs; but if you don't, EMR will create it for you. Now, your browser screen will look as follows:

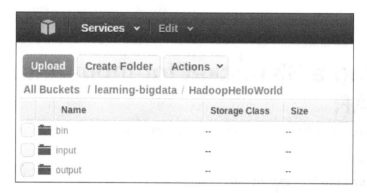

4. Click on the folder named `input`, and then click on **Upload**. A pop up comes up with options to upload files. Click on **Add Files** to open up the file browser. Select the input file(s). In our case, select the sample input file named `sample1.csv` as used in the previous chapter.

   Let's now look at the browser screen which will look as follows:

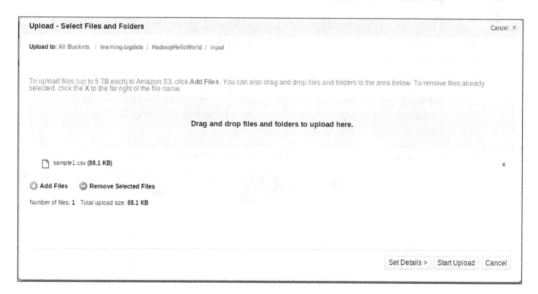

5. Now, click on **Start Upload**. Follow the instructions to upload the JAR file in the `bin` folder.

Now, we are all set to launch an EMR cluster to execute our `Hello World` solution created in the previous chapter.

How to launch an EMR cluster

The following are the tools provided by AWS to launch an EMR cluster:

- AWS management console
- CLI tools
- SDKs available for a range of programming languages

In this chapter, we will use the first method, that is, we will launch an EMR cluster from the AWS management console. You will get to know about the second method in *Chapter 8, Amazon EMR – Command-line Interface Client*, which would take up the command-line tool available to be used with EMR.

Perform the following steps to launch an EMR cluster and add the Job Step to execute our `HadoopHelloWorld` problem.

Step 1 – Opening the Elastic MapReduce dashboard

Log in to your AWS management console and go to the EMR Dashboard by navigating to **Services** | **All AWS Services** | **Elastic MapReduce**. From the top-right corner, select the region in which you want your cluster to be launched. Also make sure that you have an EC2 key pair generated for this region.

Step 2 – Creating an EMR cluster

Click on **Create Cluster**. This will open up a page, wherein you can configure the cluster and provide various other parameters along with bootstrap actions and add Job Steps to be executed by this cluster.

Step 3 – The cluster configuration

Create the cluster configuration. The following very basic configurations are set in this section:

- **Cluster name**: You should give any suitable name to the cluster.

- **Termination protection**: As we discussed in *Chapter 4*, *Amazon EMR – Hadoop on Amazon Web Services*, by enabling termination protection, your clusters will be prevented from accidental terminations. Also, with this feature enabled to terminate the cluster, you must turn it off from your AWS management console.

- **Logging**: A cluster generates several types of logs. These include step logs, Hadoop logs, bootstrap action logs, and instance state logs, among others. By default, these logs are stored in the master node. By enabling logging, you can configure periodic archiving of these logs from the master node to S3.

- **Log folder S3 location**: If you enable logging, you need to provide the location on one of your S3 buckets where EMR will archive the logs.

- **Debugging**: EMR provides a clean user interface to browse the log files from the console. If you enable debugging on a cluster, in addition to archiving the log files to S3, it indexes those files. You can browse the step, job, task, and task attempt logs for the cluster.

The following screenshot shows a sample cluster configuration:

Step 4 – Tagging an EMR cluster

You may add up to 10 tags to your EMR cluster. Basically, these tags will be attached with the EC2 machines that will be launched as part of the cluster. Let's add a tag having a key as **EMR** and value as **HadoopHelloWorld-Test**, as shown in the following screenshot:

Step 5 – The software configuration

In this step, you need to decide which Hadoop distribution you want to use. Currently, these are the following two options:

- Amazon's Hadoop distribution
- MapR's Hadoop distribution

We will use the Amazon's Hadoop distribution. It is based on Apache Hadoop and has patches and improvements added to it in order to make it work more efficiently within the AWS environment and communicate better with other AWS services.

Amazon EMR provides you with multiple versions of Hadoop to choose from. Amazon keeps on updating this list with the latest releases of Apache Hadoop. You need to select the AMI version as per the Hadoop version you want to launch your cluster with. As discussed in the previous chapter, we have created our solution to work on Hadoop 2.2.0; hence, let's select **3.0.4 (hadoop 2.2.0)** from the dropdown, as shown in the following screenshot:

You may notice that **Hive** and **Pig** are by default added to be installed on the cluster. Remove them as we only need to have a Hadoop distribution installed on our cluster. Remove these two by clicking on the cross sign to the right of each row, as shown in the following screenshot:

Step 6 – The hardware configuration

In this step, you need to set the networking and hardware configuration for your cluster. Here you need to specify a number and type of EC2 instances you want your cluster to start with.

The following configuration can be set in this section.

Network

If you are processing sensitive data, you can choose to launch your cluster within an AWS VPC (Virtual Private Cloud). For the purpose of our *Hello World* solution test, let's leave this option to have the default value of **Launch into EC2-classic**.

EC2 availability zone

Within the selected region on which you are launching the cluster, you have the option to choose the availability zone in which you want your cluster to be launched. Let's leave the default option of **No preference** selected. You may select any availability zone of your choice.

EC2 instance(s) configurations

You have to decide on the instance type, count, and whether you want to use spot instances or not. As we have discussed in *Chapter 4, Amazon EMR – Hadoop on Amazon Web Services*, EMR provides the following three different groups of instances:

* **Master**
* **Core**
* **Task**

Using the AWS management console, the smallest type of instance that can be selected as Master is **m1.medium**. For the purpose of our test, let's have master as **m1.medium**. As our test is not going to process huge amounts of data, you should have no machine in **Core** and **Task** groups, that is, have their count should be set as 0. Your settings should look like the following screenshot:

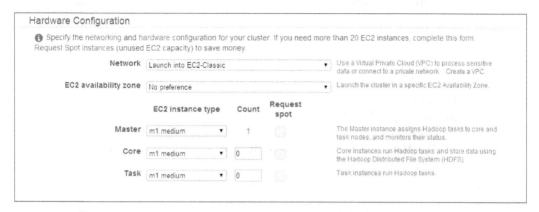

You may also request spot instances for each instance group, but spot instances can be taken away from you if the average market price goes up more than that of your bid price. Hence, it is not recommended to use spot instances as the master node. Also, it is advised that you should have a small percentage of on-demand instances for the **Core** group. For the rest of the nodes, use spot instances and keep them as part of the **Task** group.

Step 7 – Security and access

In this section, you need to select the EC2 key pair that we created earlier. Using this key pair, you can SSH into the master node of your cluster:

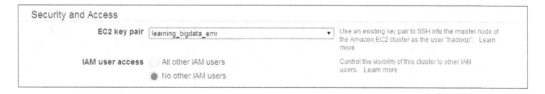

As in the previous screenshot, leave other values to default in this section.

You can also provide one or more bootstrap actions, which are scripts that are executed by EMR on every node before setting up Hadoop on them. Let's skip the section on bootstrap actions for now; we will learn about this in our next chapter.

Step 8 – Adding Job Steps

As we discussed in *Chapter 4, Amazon EMR – Hadoop on Amazon Web Services*, you can add Job Steps to your EMR cluster, and EMR executes them one by one in sequential order in the order these Job Steps were submitted. Your Job Step can be one of the following five options provided by EMR right now:

- Custom JAR
- Streaming program
- Hive program
- Pig program
- Impala program

You will select **Custom JAR** as we are going to execute the custom JAR we have created in the previous chapter:

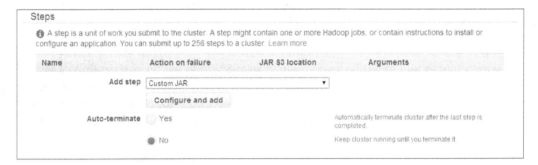

Now, click on **Configure and add**. A pop up will be shown to you that can configure your job step. The following four parameters can be configured here:

- **Name of the step**: You should provide an appropriate name for this Job Step. Let's keep it `HadoopHelloWorld Test`.

- **S3 location of your JAR file**: This is the key in the S3 location of the JAR file where you have uploaded your custom JAR, as discussed in our earlier section. It should resemble something like `s3://learning-bigdata/HadoopHelloWorld/bin/hits-by-country.jar`.

- **Arguments to your JAR**: This is an optional field. Here you will provide the arguments for the custom JAR; the same arguments that we had passed to our custom JAR while executing it locally in the previous chapter. You can have the following value:

  ```
  -D mapred.textoutputformat.separator=,  s3://learning-bigdata/
  HadoopHelloWorld/input/sample1.csv  s3://learning-bigdata/
  HadoopHelloWorld/output/1/
  ```

- **Action that EMR should take on the failure of your step**: The default value for this parameter is to continue executing other jobs in the queue. As discussed in *Chapter 4*, *Amazon EMR – Hadoop on Amazon Web Services*, you might want to change the parameter to **Cancel and wait** if you have jobs dependent on the previous job's success.

After filling all these details for the Job Step, you will have something similar to what is shown in the following screenshot:

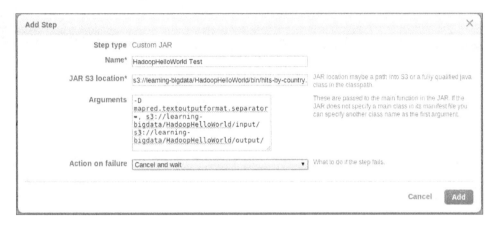

Now, click on **Add** to add your Job Step.

One last configuration you have to do is to decide whether you want your cluster to be automatically terminated after the Job Step is completed. For now, it is recommended to select **No** and keep the cluster running until you explicitly terminate it. This is to allow you to add more steps and test various other things. Also, what if the Job Step fails? You should have the chance to correct it and add another step. Anyway, this test step will be finished within a few minutes and AWS bills per hour, so you can keep the cluster up for at least an hour, as shown in the following screenshot:

You are all set to create your cluster now. Click on **Create cluster** on the right-bottom corner to create the cluster with the configurations you have done till now.

Your cluster will be launched and you will be taken to the **Cluster Details** page of the newly launched cluster. It may take up to 5 minutes for your cluster to bootstrap itself.

As we have discussed in *Chapter 4, Amazon EMR – Hadoop on Amazon Web Services*, a launched cluster will go through a set of states. You can see the current state of the cluster at the top, just beside the cluster name. You may notice the state transition of your cluster from **Starting** to **Bootstrapping** to **Running**, as shown in the following screenshot:

Your Job Step should be completed within a couple of minutes. You can check out the collapsible **Steps** section. You can see two Job Steps: the one that you had added and the other one that was added by EMR to set up Hadoop debugging.

When you click on **View logs** for your Job Steps, the following four types of logs can be viewed to the right of the AWS management console:

- `controller`: This log file has the information about the processing of this particular step. If your step fails while loading, you can find the stack trace in this log. For example, if your JAR file's path is incorrect or your output directory already exists, these kinds of logs can be found in this file.
- `syslog`: This log has the description of the execution of Hadoop jobs in the step.
- `stderr`: This contains the output to the standard error channel of Hadoop while it processes the step.
- `stdout`: This contains the output to the standard output channel of Hadoop while it processes the step.

At this point, your Job Steps section should look as follows:

If you want, you can try to execute this same JAR over other input files or add any of your other solutions as a Job Step. But if you are done with it, do not forget to terminate the cluster.

 Do not forget to terminate your cluster.

In order to terminate your cluster, click on **Terminate**, as shown in the following screenshot:

You will be prompted with a confirmation message stating the following:

Are you sure you want to terminate this cluster?

Any pending work or data residing on the cluster will be lost, such as data stored in HDFS. This action is irreversible.

If you are sure that no job is running on the cluster and that you are done with testing and playing around with this cluster, you can click on **Terminate** on the pop-up confirmation box.

Viewing results

Now that we have successfully executed our HadoopHelloWorld Job Step on EMR, we should check out the output.

You should log in to your AWS management console and go to the S3 dashboard. Here, you will browse to the output location you had given in the arguments while adding the Job Step to the cluster.

You should see two files being created in your output location, as shown in the following screenshot:

Hadoop's MapReduce runtime creates a _SUCCESS file in the output directory on the successful completion of a job. This is useful as it makes it easy for applications that are going to consume this output to decide that the complete result set is present or it will wait.

Also, the second file you see there is named part-r-00000. The output files are named as part-x-yyyyy, where:

- x is either m or r, depending on whether the output is written directly from a mapper (by a map-only job) or a reducer.
- yyyyy is the mapper or reducer task number.
- Now, you should select **part-r-00000** and navigate to **Actions | Download**. Open this file in your favorite editor. You should find the output as follows:

  China,819

  India,1142

  UK,633

  US,932

- This is the same output we saw in the previous chapter where we executed it locally.

Summary

We have successfully launched an EMR cluster and executed the `HadoopHelloWorld` solution we created in the previous chapter. We also learned how to create an EC2 key pair and how to upload files to S3.

You can connect to the master node via SSH using the EC2 key pair. You can open an SSH tunnel to the master, and by coupling that with browser proxy tools or plugins, you can even access websites such as the web view of the NameNode and the ResourceManager that are hosted on the master node. We will learn about all these in our next chapter along with some of the advanced configurations you can do while launching an EMR cluster.

7
Amazon EMR – Cluster Management

In this chapter, we will learn about EMR cluster management including different mechanisms for managing EMR clusters, troubleshooting, and performance tuning. We will look at how you can connect to the master node of an EMR cluster along with learning how to access the various web views provided by Hadoop. We will also become familiar with accessing different logs provided by EMR for troubleshooting and debugging purposes.

EMR cluster management – different methods

Amazon EMR provides a hosted Hadoop, Pig, Hive, and Hbase services for developers and businesses to help them build Big Data applications without worrying about the deployment complexity or managing Hadoop clusters with scalable underlying infrastructure. We have learned the benefits of Amazon EMR in *Chapter 4, Amazon EMR – Hadoop on Amazon Web Services*. In this section, we will look at the different ways of managing an Amazon EMR cluster.

We can access the AWS EMR service using multiple ways as listed:

- **Web console (AWS management console)**: This is a web interface to access all Amazon Web Service offerings. It can be used to launch EMR jobs and manage them. The AWS management console is an easy-to-use interface for developers who are not very familiar with using **command-line interface (CLI)** or programmatic SDK. We saw how to use the AWS management console to launch an EMR cluster in *Chapter 6, Executing Hadoop Jobs on an Amazon EMR Cluster*.

- **AWS SDK**: This SDK provides functions to access EMR features using popular languages such as Java, Python, .NET, and many more. We can launch, manage, or customize EMR clusters using SDK.

- **CLI tools**: These are client-side tools, which can be installed on your computer to access EMR services and manage jobs. They are very useful while building automated jobs for launching EMR clusters or terminating them on a need basis using scripted automation.

 We will see how to use the CLI tools provided by AWS to launch, monitor, and manage an EMR cluster in *Chapter 8, Amazon EMR – Command-line Interface Client*.

- **WebService API**: Amazon provides low-level API access to EMR features for custom integration or building a specific toolkit for your business needs. This will be useful for programmatic integration into your existing product or application.

The following table compares the functionalities of the Amazon EMR interfaces:

Feature	Console	CLI	API, SDK, and libraries
Launch multiple clusters	Yes	Yes	Yes
Define bootstrap actions in a cluster	Yes	Yes	Yes
View logs for Hadoop jobs, tasks and task attempts using a graphical interface	Yes		
Implement Hadoop data processing programmatically			Yes
Monitor clusters in real time	Yes		
Provide verbose cluster details		Yes	Yes
Resize running clusters	Yes	Yes	Yes
Run clusters with multiple steps		Yes	Yes
Specify the MapReduce executable in multiple computer languages	Yes	Yes	Yes
Transfer data to and from Amazon S3 automatically	Yes	Yes	Yes
Terminate clusters in real time	Yes	Yes	

EMR bootstrap actions

Suppose you want some specific software installed on the machines executing your Hadoop jobs, or if you want to tweak some of the default Hadoop configurations, EMR bootstrap actions will help you perform these tasks.

Amazon EMR provides a mechanism to customize the installation and configuration of Hadoop clusters using bootstrap actions. A bootstrap action is a script that will be run on the cluster before Hadoop starts and a node is ready for data processing.

EMR provides certain default bootstrap actions like Hadoop configuration customization, so you can tweak or tune the default Hadoop parameters of their cluster. However, you can create custom bootstrap actions based on your requirements.

We need to store the bootstrap actions in the S3 bucket and one cluster can have up to 16 bootstrap actions. They will be executed in the order of their assignment while launching the cluster.

> If a bootstrap action script returns a nonzero error code, then EMR considers it to be a failure and will terminate the entire cluster. However, if only a few nodes return an error while executing the bootstrap action, then AWS EMR will try to launch replacement instances in the cluster.

We can add bootstrap actions from the AWS management console, CLI, or EMR SDK.

When you launch an EMR cluster from the management console, you will have the following five options while adding a bootstrap action:

- **Configure Hadoop**
- **Configure daemons**
- **Memory intensive configuration**
- **Run if**
- **Custom action**

These options are shown in the following screenshot:

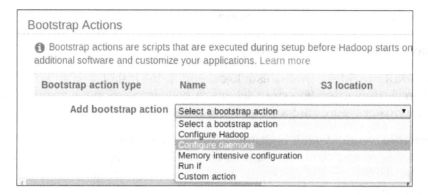

Every bootstrap action is ultimately a program/script that should be located somewhere in S3, which your clusters can access and execute on your behalf while launching an EMR cluster. As you can see from the list of options EMR provides for bootstrap action, in addition for you to add a custom action, it also has a set of predefined bootstrap actions which you can use. Each bootstrap action also takes a list of arguments that depends on the bootstrap program as well as your requirements.

Let's take a look at each one of these options.

Configuring Hadoop

This bootstrap option allows you to customize Hadoop configurations for an entire cluster. The program (script) for this is located at `s3://elasticmapreduce/bootstrap-actions/configure-hadoop`.

You can either provide the XML file having Hadoop configurations overriding the existing default configuration files or you can just set a key-value pair for some specific Hadoop configurations. In accordance with this, there are two type of arguments this script accepts:

- `--keyword-config-file`: You can specify a S3 or local location of a Hadoop configuration file. It merges the default configurations with the configuration you have provided in your XML configuration file. This file should be a valid Hadoop configuration file.

- `--keyword-key-value`: Using this option, you can override specific key-value pairs in the default Hadoop configurations.

There are many categories in which Hadoop configurations are divided and each of them is specified in a separate XML configuration file. The `--keyword` portion of the options denotes which category of configuration you are specifying. The following table shows the list of these configuration types and the file in which these configurations are expected to be:

Configuration file name	`--keyword`	File name shortcut	Key-value pair shortcut
`core-site.xml`	`core`	C	c
`hdfs-site.xml`	`hdfs`	H	h
`mapred-site.xml`	`mapred`	M	m
`yarn-site.xml`	`yarn`	Y	y

So, if you want to override any configurations in the `mapred-site.xml` file, and assuming that your configuration file is located at `s3://myCustomConfig/mapred-site.xml`, your arguments will look like one of the following:

- `--mapred-config-file s3://myCustomConfig/mapred-site.xml`
- `-M s3://myCustomConfig/mapred-site.xml`

You can also provide a key-value pair along with a file; in this case, if any configuration is repeated, then the later one will override the earlier ones.

For example, let's assume that your configuration file has the following entry:

```
<?xml version="1.0" encoding="UTF-8"?>
<?xml-stylesheet type="text/xsl" href="configuration.xsl"?>
<configuration>
    <property>
        <name>mapred.child.java.opts</name>
        <value>-Xmx256m</value>
    </property>
</configuration>
```

You provide the following argument to your Configure Hadoop bootstrap action:

`-M s3://myCustomConfig/mapred-site.xml -m mapred.child.java.opts '-Xmx512m'`

In this case, the setting in the file will be overridden by the key-pair provided after you set up the same configuration in the configuration file.

So, if you want to configure Hadoop while launching an EMR cluster, in the bootstrap actions section, you will choose the **Configure Hadoop** option and click on **Configure and add**. You will get a popup where you can provide the location of your configuration file and/or the configuration key-value pairs, as shown in the following screenshot:

Configuring daemons

There are many daemons which collectively form the entire execution system of Hadoop. This bootstrap action allows you to configure the heap size or other advanced JVM options for these Hadoop daemons. The program (script) for this is located at `s3://elasticmapreduce/bootstrap-actions/configure-daemons`.

There are three types of arguments this script expects:

- `--daemon-heap-size`: This allows you to set the heap size in megabytes for the specified daemon
- `--daemon-opts`: This allows you to set additional Java options for the specified daemon
- `--replace`: This allows you to replace the existing `hadoop-user-env.sh` file

The `--daemon` portion of these options denotes the daemon for which the configuration is to be applied. The following table lists the daemons for Hadoop-1.x and Hadoop-2.x:

Hadoop 1.x	Hadoop 2.x
namenode	namenode
datanode	datanode

Hadoop 1.x	Hadoop 2.x
jotracker	resourcemanager
tasktracker	nodemanager
client	client

Say you want to provide the cluster's namenode a heap size of 1 GB (1024 MB) and want it to use parallel GC, you can use this bootstrap action with the following arguments:

```
--namenode-heap-size=1024 --namenode-opts="-XX:-UseParallelGC"
```

 The `--client-heap-size` option does not work with Hadoop-1.x. If you want to set the heap size to 1024 MB, you need to use `--client-opts="-Xmx1024"`.

Run if

EMR holds node settings in the `instance.json` file and cluster configuration in `job-flow.json`. It provides you with a predefined bootstrap action using which you can run a command conditionally when any value you provide is present in `instance.json` or in `job-flow.json`.

The command you specify can also be a file on S3 that EMR can download and execute. Let's say that you have a script at `s3://myCustomCommand/command.sh` that you want to execute only on the master node. You can use this bootstrap action with the following arguments:

```
instance.isMaster=true s3://myCustomCommand/command.sh
```

The following table lists the parameters present in the node settings file, `instance.json`:

Parameter	Hadoop version
isMaster	1.x, 2.x
isRunningNameNode	1.x, 2.x
isRunningDataNode	1.x, 2.x
isRunningJobTracker	1.x, 2.x
isRunningTaskTracker	1.x, 2.x
isRunningResourceManager	2.x
isRunningNodeManager	2.x

All the parameters are self-explanatory. They are all of Boolean type and either have `true` or `false` as their value.

The following table lists the parameters present in the cluster configuration file, `job-flow.json`:

Parameter	Type	Description
JobFlowID	String	The job flow ID of the cluster
jobFlowCreationInstant	Long	The time when a cluster was created
instanceCount	Integer	Number of nodes in an instance group
masterInstanceID	String	The ID of the master node
masterPrivateDnsName	String	The private DNS of the master node
masterInstanceType	String	The instance type of the master node
slaveInstanceType	String	The instance type of the slave node
HadoopVersion	String	The Hadoop version running on the cluster
instanceGroups		This is a list of objects having the details of each of the instance groups in the cluster

Additionally, each entry in the list of values for `instanceGroups` has the following details:

- `instanceGroupId`
- `instanceGroupName`
- `instanceRole` (this can be one of `Master`, `Core`, or `Task`)
- `instanceType`
- `requestedInstanceCount`

Memory-intensive configuration

EMR has a predefined bootstrap action that configures your cluster to take on memory-intensive workloads. It takes the instance types in your cluster into consideration and accordingly sets the following Hadoop variables (from `hadoop-user-env.sh`) and configurations:

- `HADOOP_JOBTRACKER_HEAPSIZE`
- `HADOOP_NAMENODE_HEAPSIZE`
- `HADOOP_TASKTRACKER_HEAPSIZE`
- `HADOOP_DATANODE_HEAPSIZE`
- `mapred.child.java.opts`

- `mapred.tasktracker.map.tasks.maximum`
- `mapred.tasktracker.reduce.tasks.maximum`

 You might not need to use this bootstrap action because from AMI 2.0.0 and later, the memory-intensive settings are set by default. If you do not need memory-intensive configurations, then you can use the **Configure Hadoop** and/or **Configure daemon** actions to tune your cluster's configurations accordingly.

Custom action

You can have any custom script executed as a bootstrap action. You just need to provide the valid S3 location of your script. Additionally, you can also specify arguments accepted by your script, if any.

Say, you have your custom bootstrap script at `s3://myCustomAction/action.sh` and it accepts two arguments, you would add it as shown in the following screenshot:

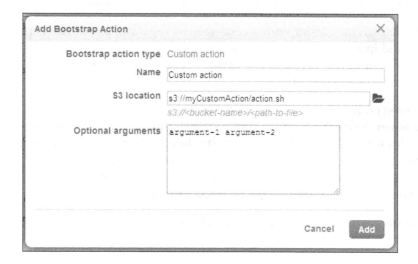

 You can use custom bootstrap actions to install third-party software such as Ganglia for monitoring the cluster performance. The location for the script to install and set up Ganglia is `s3://elasticmapreduce/bootstrap-actions/install-ganglia`. It does not accept any argument.

EMR cluster monitoring and troubleshooting

We can use one of the tools (web console, CLI, SDK, or API) to get EMR cluster details in AWS. The web console displays all of the clusters you've launched in the past two weeks (both active and terminated).

We have seen in the previous chapter that if you click on a cluster name, then the web console displays a **Details** pane with information about that cluster. As we will see in our next chapter, we can also find the details about a cluster from the CLI using the `--describe` argument along with a Job Flow ID.

EMR cluster logging

Amazon EMR and Hadoop both generate logfiles as the cluster begins execution. You can access these logfiles from several different tools, depending on the configuration specified when we launch the cluster.

Every cluster publishes log files to the `/mnt/var/log/` directory on the master node. These logfiles are only available while the cluster is running.

When you launch the cluster with an Amazon S3 log path, the cluster copies the logfiles stored in `/mnt/var/log/` on the master node to the Amazon S3 bucket location in five-minute intervals. This ensures that you have access to the logfiles even after the cluster is terminated.

We have seen earlier that EMR cluster generates multiple logfiles that can be accessed when the cluster is in the active state. However, if you would like to persist these logfiles for further analysis after cluster termination, then you need to launch the cluster with logging enabled from the AWS web console or with the `--log-uri` option from the EMR CLI toolkit. When you enable persistent logging for the EMR cluster, it requires the location of the S3 bucket for storing cluster logs.

The following sections describe the different types of logfiles generated by an EMR cluster.

Hadoop logs

These are the standard logfiles generated by Apache Hadoop and stored in `/mnt/var/log/hadoop/` on the master node. They contain information about Hadoop jobs, MapReduce tasks, and task attempts.

Bootstrap action logs

When an EMR cluster is launched with bootstrap actions, the execution of bootstrap action are logged. These logfiles are stored in `/mnt/var/log/bootstrap-actions/` on the master node of the cluster. If we have multiple bootstrap actions, then each action logs its results in a separate subdirectory such as `/mnt/var/log/bootstrap-actions/1/` for the first bootstrap action, `/mnt/var/log/bootstrap-actions/2/` for the second bootstrap action, and likewise.

Job Step logs

These logs are generated by the Amazon EMR service for each of the Job Steps and contain information about the cluster. These logfiles are stored in the `/mnt/var/log/hadoop/steps/` directory on the master node of the cluster. Each of the Job Steps logs its results in a separate subdirectory such as `/mnt/var/log/hadoop/steps/1/` for the first step, `/mnt/var/log/hadoop/steps/2/` for the second step, and likewise.

Cluster instance state logs

These logs provide information about the system health metrics such as CPU, memory, and garbage collector threads of the node. The logfiles are stored in `/mnt/var/log/instance-state/` on the master node. You can also access the instance health metrics of an active cluster using the CloudWatch service.

Connecting to the master node

In order to connect to the master node of your EMR cluster via SSH, you need two things:

- The master node's public DNS name, which you can get from the cluster details on the AWS management console.

- The private key file for the EC2 key pair you had used while launching the cluster. In *Chapter 6*, *Executing Hadoop Jobs on an Amazon EMR Cluster*, we saw how to create and use an EC2 key pair while launching the cluster.

Connect to your cluster's master node using the following command:

```
ssh -i <path-to-private-key-file> hadoop@<master-public-DNS-name>
```

For example, say, your private key file path is `/home/user/keys/learning_bigdata_emr.pem` and your cluster's master has the DNS name as `ec2-108-22-59-61.compute-1.amazonaws.com`, then you would SSH to your master using the following command:

```
ssh -i /home/user/keys/learning_bigdata_emr.pem hadoop@ec2-108-22-59-61.compute-1.amazonaws.com
```

It should be noted that the path and master node's DNS name used in this example are just imaginary and should be replaced by your actual data.

> In order to provide SSH access to your master node while launching your EMR cluster, you must add your external source IP for it to be allowed to connect to the TCP port `22` (SSH). You can do this by modifying the security group.

Websites hosted on the master node

Hadoop publishes web-based user interfaces. Ganglia (a monitoring application) and other such applications also publish web interfaces. These are websites hosted on the master node. Due to security reasons, these websites aren't open to the public and can only be accessed via the local web server in the master node.

The following table lists the various web interfaces Hadoop provides:

Name of the interface	URL	Hadoop version
ResourceManager	`http://<master-public-dns-name>:9026/`	2.x
HDFS NameNode	`http://<master-public-dns-name>:9101/`	1.x and 2.x
NodeManager	`http://<master-public-dns-name>:9035/`	2.x
JobTracker	`http://<master-public-dns-name>:9100/`	1.x
TaskTracker	`http://<master-public-dns-name>:9103/`	1.x

There are multiple ways you can access these websites:

- Connect to the master node via SSH and use a text-based web browser to access these websites. You can use the Lynx text browser. If you are running Hadoop 2.x, then you can view the web interface for the ResourceManager by using the following command:

  ```
  lynx http://localhost:9026
  ```

Though it is the easiest and fastest way to view these websites, it has a very limited user interface and cannot display graphics.

- Create an SSH tunnel to the master node and configure your browser to use a SOCKS proxy for all URLs. How to configure this depends on the browser; hence, you can consult your browser's documentation for details.

- Create an SSH tunnel to the master node and use a browser plugin such as FoxyProxy (available for Google Chrome, Mozilla FireFox, and Internet Explorer). It allows you to filter URLs based on user-defined text patterns and uses a SOCKS proxy only for the URLs that match those patterns.

It is recommended to use the third option as once installed and configured, it automatically uses the SOCKS proxy when you browse websites from your master node and turn off the proxy while you browse other websites on the Internet. We will see in a bit how to configure it, but first let's see how to create an SSH tunnel to the master node.

Creating an SSH tunnel to the master node

As with connecting to the master node, you will need the private key file of the EC2 key pair as well as the DNS name of the master node of your cluster.

Now, in order to create an SSH tunnel from your local machine to the master node of your cluster, execute the following command:

```
ssh –i <path-to-private-key-file> -ND <port-number> hadoop@<master-node-public-DNS-name>
```

For example, say, your private key file path is /home/user/keys/learning_bigdata_emr.pem and your cluster's master has the DNS name as ec2-108-22-59-61.compute-1.amazonaws.com, then you would create an SSH to your master using the following command:

```
ssh –i /home/user/keys/learning_bigdata_emr.pem –ND 8157 hadoop@ec2-108-22-59-61.compute-1.amazonaws.com
```

 Whatever <port-number> you provide here should be used while creating the proxy configurations on your browser.

Configuring FoxyProxy

FoxyProxy is a popular browser plugin that provides various proxy management tools. It is now available for Google Chrome, Mozilla Firefox, and Internet Explorer. You can configure it to use a proxy server based on URLs matching patterns that you can define.

If you have created an SSH tunnel to the master node, you can configure FoxyProxy to use it as a SOCKS proxy to connect to the websites hosted on the master node based on the URL pattern of the public DNS name of an Amazon EC2 instance (master node is also an EC2 instance).

Let's see how to install and set up FoxyProxy in Google Chrome.

Installing FoxyProxy in Google Chrome

The following steps will guide you to install FoxyProxy in Google Chrome:

1. Go to `http://getfoxyproxy.org/downloads.html` and click on the **Standard** version for Chrome.

2. This will take you to the web store of Google Chrome listing **FoxyProxy Standard**. Click on **Free** and then on the pop-up confirmation, click on **Add**.

3. This plugin should now be successfully added to your Google Chrome browser and you should be able to access it from the top-right corner just beside the address bar, as shown in the following screenshot:

Creating a proxy setting

To create a proxy setting, perform the following steps:

1. Click on the FoxyProxy plugin icon and select **Options**. This will take you to the FoxyProxy's **Extension** tab.

2. Click on **Add New Proxy**. This will bring up a pop up, where you can provide the required parameters to create your proxy setting.

3. Click on the **General** tab and enter a name for this proxy setting, say, name it `AWSProxy` as shown in the following screenshot:

4. Click on the **Proxy Details** tab and select **Manual Proxy Configuration**. Now, perform the following settings:

    1. As you have created the `SOCKS` proxy (an SSH tunnel) on your local machine on `<port number>`, say 8157, enter `localhost` in the **Host or IP Address** field and 8157 in the **Port** field.

    2. Tick the **SOCKS proxy?** checkbox.

    3. Select **SOCKS v5.**

    These settings are shown in the following screenshot:

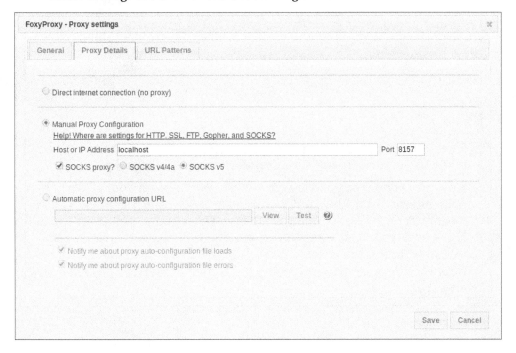

5. Click on the **URL Patterns** tab. Now you need to add patterns so that any URL having a text pattern, `*ec2*.amazonaws.com*`, `*ec2.internal*`, or `*.compute.internal*` will use this proxy.

6. Click on **Add New Pattern** and perform the following settings:

    1. Select the **Enabled** checkbox.

    2. Provide a suitable name for the pattern.

    3. Enter the following URL pattern in the **URL pattern** box: `*ec2*.amazonaws.com*`.

    4. Under **URL Inclusion/Exclusion**, select **Whitelist**.

    5. Under **Pattern Contains**, select **Wildcards**.

    6. Click on **OK**.

   Similarly add other patterns as well. After performing these settings, you will get the following screen:

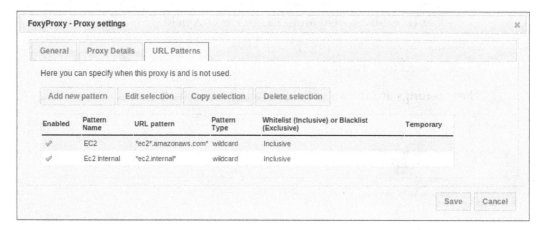

7. Now in the **Extensions** home tab, click on the options for **Proxy mode** and select **Use proxies based on their predefined patterns and priorities**.

8. Now, you should be good to access websites hosted on your cluster's master node directly from your local machine's browser using the public DNS of the master node. So, assuming that your master node's public DNS name is `ec2-108-22-59-61.compute-1.amazonaws.com`, you can access the web interface for the ResourceManager by entering the following address from your browser: `http://ec2-108-22-59-61.compute-1.amazonaws.com:9026`.

9. You should see a web view, as shown in the following screenshot:

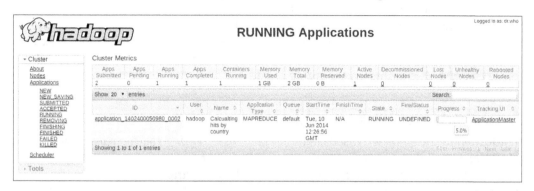

You can refer to the AWS documentation for the steps to set up FoxyProxy in Firefox available at `http://docs.aws.amazon.com/ ElasticMapReduce/latest/DeveloperGuide/emr-connect- master-node-proxy.html`.

EMR cluster performance monitoring

When we are using Amazon EMR for Hadoop programming, we want to track MapReduce tasks' progress and know the health metrics of different nodes in the cluster. For this purpose, EMR provides several tools to monitor the performance of EMR clusters.

Each Hadoop cluster publishes a set of web interfaces on the master node that contain information about the cluster. We can access these web interfaces by using an SSH tunnel to connect them on the master node or by allowing all traffic to the master node from your network by configuring AWS security groups. The Hadoop job tracker UI console can be accessed on the master node at the default http port of `9100` to look at the internal metrics of map/reduce executions.

Also, EMR cluster reports metrics to the CloudWatch service in AWS. CloudWatch is a web service that tracks metrics that can be used to define alarms on those metrics. Those alarms can be delivered to your e-mail as notifications. Some of the metrics provided by EMR using CloudWatch include a number of map tasks, reduce tasks, pending map/reduce tasks, HDFS utilization, HDFS bytes read, HDFS bytes written, S3 bytes read, S3 bytes written, Jobs Status, Jobs Pending, and so on.

However, sometimes we want to have granular monitoring data for the entire cluster including node-level health metrics such as CPU, disk, network, and others, so EMR supports using Ganglia as a cluster monitoring tool. To use Ganglia, we have to install it on the cluster using bootstrap actions. After successful installation, we can monitor various health metrics of the cluster by using an SSH tunnel to connect it to the Ganglia UI running on the master node.

Adding Ganglia to a cluster

In addition to the steps we discussed in *Chapter 6, Executing Hadoop Jobs on an Amazon EMR Cluster*, while you are launching an EMR cluster from the AWS management console, you can install Ganglia in your cluster by choosing **Ganglia** under the **Additional Applications** list and click on **Configure and add**. That's all, a fantastic monitoring tool will be installed for you to use.

Ganglia also publishes a web interface to the local web server of the master node; hence, you need to follow the same path you did in order to access the Hadoop websites hosted on the master node. That is, create an SSH tunnel and use FoxyProxy to set up a SOCKS proxy. You can access Ganglia's web interface by entering the following URL from your browser: http://<master-node-public-DNS-name>/ganglia.

The section <master-node-public-DNS-name> in the mentioned URL should be replaced by your master node's public DNS name.

Ganglia's web interface's home page has the overview of the cluster's performance having graphs related to the following four major metrics:

- **Cluster Load**
- **Cluster Memory**
- **Cluster CPU**
- **Cluster Network**

Just below the four graphs, you can see one graph each for the number of nodes in your cluster. The default metric for which these graphs are shown is **Load**. You can change that from the **Metric** dropdown.

You can get a detailed set of statistics for a given node by selecting the node from the related dropdown or by clicking on the corresponding node-instance graph. This will take you to the **Host Overview** page of the node.

Ganglia also reports Hadoop-related metrics for each node. These metrics are prefixed by their category:

- Distributed filesystem (dfs.*)
- Java virtual machine (jvm.*)
- Mapreduce (mapred.*)
- Remote procedure calls (rpc.*)

You can see the complete list of metrics by clicking on the **Gmetrics** link on the **Host Overview** page.

EMR cluster debugging – console

The AWS management console provides a **Debug** button that can be used to open an interface to browse an archived copy of the logfiles stored in an Amazon S3 bucket. When you launch a cluster with debugging enabled, Amazon EMR creates an index of those logfiles. When you click on **Debug**, it provides a graphical interface that you can use to browse the indexed logfiles.

EMR best practices

In this section, we will see some of the best practices you should follow while using EMR.

Data transfer

If you need to read a lot of data from S3, then it's recommended to use the s3DistCP utility to copy data into the local HDFS for analysis instead of directly reading from S3 to improve the performance. The s3DistCP utility is provided by AWS and it can be scheduled as a first step of your Job Flow to copy data from S3 to the local HDFS for further analysis by the next set of jobs in the Job Flow.

If you have large data to be moved from the local HDFS to S3 for persistence or save results before terminating a transient cluster, then look at the Jets3t toolkit. It provides various tools including data synchronization to move data from local directories to S3. It is ideal for performing data backups to S3.

Also, Aspera Direct-to-S3 is a toolkit-based on proprietary file transfer implementation using UDP to move large amounts of data over the Internet at very high speeds. It can be used to move data from on-premise to AWS or from existing HDFS to S3.

Data compression

Compression is one of the most quick and effective ways to reduce the data size in S3 to lower AWS costs and also reduce data transfer time to move data around. Also, data compression can be used between different MapReduce jobs while sharing data from map to reduce or from one job to other. It will be very effective if you have large intermediate data during the processing. EMR supports different compression algorithms such as gzip, lzo, snappy, and bzip2. However, gzip and snappy don't allow splitting compressed files. It might not be an effective way if your input data set contains many large compressed files.

Data compression can be enabled by setting `mapreduce.map.output.compress` to `true` and you can choose the compression algorithm to be used by setting `mapreduce.map.output.compress.codec` to a specific algorithm such as `lzo` or `snappy`.

Cluster size and instance type

AWS provides a variety of EC2 instance types to suit different workloads broadly categorized based on memory, CPU, or network types. While provisioning an EMR cluster, it's important to choose the correct instance type as some jobs are CPU bound while others may be memory or disk bound. So, it's important to benchmark your job and choose an appropriate instance type.

Also, one m3.xlarge machine will have twice the capacity of an m3.large machine, so if your cluster size is 100 and you are using m3.large instances, then you can consider using m3.xlarge to reduce the size while effectively providing the same amount of capacity for the cluster. One of the main benefits of AWS is that you can easily switch between different instance types without worrying too much about the underlying infrastructure complexity based on your business needs.

Hadoop configuration and MapReduce tuning

When you are writing MapReduce programs, it's always recommended to profile your programs on a single node before launching a cluster to execute it. Based on our requirements, we might also have to tune the default parameters of Hadoop such as the number of tasks per node, heap size of the JVM, HDFS block size, and others.

The size of your cluster depends on the number of MapReduce tasks required given the size of your input data set and HDFS block size. If you are using data compression for the files in the input dataset, then make sure these files are splittable to avoid the bottleneck of each file being processed by only one mapper.

You can use default bootstrap action to increase JVM heap size and number of map/reduce tasks per node based on sample executions or profiling data. It can help you in tuning the cluster size and type later.

Also, if your map tasks execution time takes only seconds to a minute, then you can reduce the number of mappers in the cluster to avoid the overhead of managing too many mappers. By default, the number of mappers will be computed based on the input data set size and HDFS block size; but if you have many small files, then your mapper tasks are short lived, so we should aggregate them to produce large files as part of the data ingest process.

You should also check if your mapper tasks are using disk due spill where available buffer memory for a mapper task was exhausted, so it results in data being written to a disk. In such cases, using data compression in mapper as described in an earlier section will reduce the disk I/O and improve mapper performance.

Cost optimization

AWS provides a variety of instances such as on-demand, reserved, and spot instances for EMR. Depending upon your use case of EMR cluster, you can choose going for reserved instances, where by paying a little one-time upfront fee, we will get significant discounts on the per hour billing rates.

If your EMR clusters can run for more than 17 percent of the time (in a month), then going for reserved instances will save you money. There are multiple types of reserved instances such as low, medium, and high utilization based on the usage patterns. If you have a very sporadic data analysis job using EMR, then low utilization based reserved instances would work great, or else you can look at medium or high utilization for use cases where a permanent cluster is required.

Spot instances are a spare capacity of EC2 made available to end users via real-time bidding price, where we can bid our own price for EC2 instance per hour billing and if the current spot price is lower than our bid price, then EC2 instances will be available for the usage. However, if the spot price exceeds the bid price, then instances will be taken away automatically. Since the MapReduce framework allows for failure of some nodes in the cluster and work can be reallocated to other nodes, spot instances are a good choice.

EMR uses master, core, and task nodes in the cluster for processing in which task nodes are purely for MapReduce jobs execution, so failure is acceptable unlike master node, where a failure means the entire cluster will be terminated. So, we can use spot instances as task nodes in the cluster where a failure of nodes will not affect the overall job execution but would delay the total processing time.

Summary

In this chapter, we learned some of the advanced configurations such as various different types of bootstrap actions you can add to your cluster. We also learned ways to connect to the master node and view the various web interfaces published by Hadoop. Further, we learned how to install Ganglia and access its web view in order to monitor our cluster's performance in detail.

Till now, we have used the AWS console to launch and manage an EMR cluster, but many of us like the CLI tools. In our next chapter, we will learn how to launch an EMR cluster, add steps to it, keep track of the status of each step, and finally, how to terminate the cluster, all from the command line.

8
Amazon EMR – Command-line Interface Client

The **command-line interface (CLI)** tools and commands are often preferred over the UI-based tool by experienced programmers. Also, using CLI clients, we can do things in a single command, while we might need multiple clicks in the UI-based tool. In this chapter, we will learn about EMR cluster management using the CLI client. We will go through its installation and setup and discuss the various ways in which we can use the CLI client to manage Amazon EMR clusters.

EMR – CLI client installation

CLI is a client-side tool that can be installed on your computer to access EMR services and manage the cluster. We will learn to set up this toolkit and how to use it to launch EMR clusters and execute MapReduce jobs. The EMR CLI client requires a Ruby environment to be installed, and it supports Ruby 1.8.7, 1.9.2, and 2.0 Versions.

Step 1 – Installing Ruby

Linux users can download Ruby in different versions from the following URLs:

- **Ruby 1.8.7**: `http://www.ruby-lang.org/en/news/2010/06/23/ruby-1-8-7-p299-released/`

- **Ruby 1.9.2**: `https://www.ruby-lang.org/en/news/2014/02/24/ruby-1-9-3-p545-is-released/`

- **Ruby 2.0**: `https://www.ruby-lang.org/en/news/2014/02/24/ruby-2-0-0-p451-is-released/`

Windows users can download RubyInstaller for the setup from
`http://rubyinstaller.org/downloads/`.

Mac OS X ships with a Ruby environment installed.

You can use the `ruby -v` command to check whether Ruby is installed on your
system or not, including the version details:

```
ruby 2.0.0p451 (2014-02-24 revision 45167)
[universal.x86_64-darwin13]
```

Step 2 – Installing and verifying RubyGems framework

The EMR CLI requires RubyGems Version 1.8 or later, so we need to check whether
it's installed on the system or not before proceeding further.

You can use `gem -v` to check whether RubyGems is installed or not. Linux/Mac OS
X users can download RubyGems from `https://rubygems.org/pages/download`
and extract it into a folder.

After downloading the latest version, you can use the following command to install
it from the extracted folder:

```
sudo ruby setup.rb
```

Windows users can download the development kit (DevKit) from
`http://rubyinstaller.org/downloads/` and create a new directory
called `rubygems` to extract files from the downloaded kit.

From the extracted directory, you can execute the following commands to install
RubyGems:

```
ruby dk.rb init
```

```
ruby dk.rb install
```

Ruby installation's file path needs to be added to the environment variable
of `PATH` so that it can be accessed using the Windows command line.

Step 3 – Installing an EMR CLI client

Create a new directory where you are going to install the CLI client. Give an appropriate name, for example, `emr-client`. In the command line, enter the following command to create a directory:

```
mkdir ~/emr-client
```

Now, download the Amazon EMR CLI toolkit from the following URL and save it in the new directory created:

```
http://elasticmapreduce.s3.amazonaws.com/elastic-mapreduce-ruby.zip
```

In order to install the CLI toolkit application, you only need to unzip the downloaded ZIP file:

```
cd ~/emr-client
unzip elastic-mapreduce-ruby.zip
```

Step 4 – Configuring AWS EMR credentials

After you have successfully installed the EMR CLI toolkit, you need to configure the credentials file that will be used by the CLI toolkit to calculate the signature required to authenticate requests with AWS for EMR services.

Create a file named `credentials.json` in the `emr-client` directory where we installed the EMR CLI toolkit. If the file is already present, just edit it with appropriate data. This file should have the access credentials of AWS, S3 bucket directory to store EMR logs, and AWS region information in which you would be launching the EMR cluster.

The contents of this file will be as follows:

```
{
"access_id": <AWS Access Key ID>,
"private_key": <AWS Secret Access Key>,
"key-pair": <Your key pair name>,
"key-pair-file": <The path and name of your PEM file>,
"log_uri": <A path on Amazon S3, such as,
  s3n://myBucket/emr-logs/">,
"region": <The region of your cluster, either us-east-1,
  us-west-2, ap-southeast-1, ap-southeast-2 ... >
}
```

This `.json` file requires AWS credentials (access key and secret key) to access the EMR services, and you can create a new access key and secret key with permissions to required resources such as EMR, S3, EC2, CloudWatch, and others. You can follow the tutorial on the AWS website (`http://docs.aws.amazon.com/general/latest/gr/getting-aws-sec-creds.html`) to create or view the AWS security credentials.

As we have seen in *Chapter 6, Executing Hadoop Jobs on an Amazon EMR Cluster*, Amazon EC2 uses public key cryptography to encrypt and decrypt login information of end users accessing EC2 instances. If you do not have a key pair created on AWS, refer to *Chapter 6, Executing Hadoop Jobs on an Amazon EMR Cluster*, and create a key pair, which you will use to launch and connect with EC2 machines launched as part of your EMR clusters.

You can learn more about EC2 key pairs by visiting `http://docs.aws.amazon.com/AWSEC2/latest/UserGuide/ec2-key-pairs.html#having-ec2-create-your-key-pair`.

As we have seen while launching an EMR cluster from the AWS management console, you need to provide the S3 location where various logs can be persisted by EMR for your cluster and its jobs.

A S3 bucket should have appropriate read and write permissions for the IAM users whose security credentials are used for accessing AWS services. To change the permissions, right-click on the S3 bucket name and select the **Properties** option. It shows the **Permissions** section where we can grant the required permissions to the IAM users on this bucket.

Step 5 – SSH access setup and configuration

After the successful setup of the EMR CLI with the required credentials configured, you have to set up SSH access to the EMR cluster using the key pair for accessing the instances in an EMR cluster.

As we have seen earlier, you need SSH access to log in to the master node of an EMR cluster, so just make sure that the private key file (the `.pem` file) has the limited permission allowed by SSH clients.

On Linux/Mac OS X, we need to switch to the directory where you have the private key file and execute the following command to set the right permissions for the `.pem` file:

```
chmod og-rwx learning_bigdata_emr.pem
```

 Windows users need to download the PuTTY software for SSH access to the master node. After installing PuTTY, we need to use the `puttygen` utility to convert the key pair file from the `.pem` format to the `.ppk` format. You can download PuTTY from http://www.chiark.greenend.org.uk/~sgtatham/putty/download.html and FAQs are available at http://www.chiark.greenend.org.uk/~sgtatham/putty/faq.html.

Step 6 – Verifying the EMR CLI installation

Now, we are ready to test CLI toolkit to access AWS EMR services. You can use the following commands to check whether we are able to access AWS EMR APIs or not:

```
cd ~/emr-client/
```

```
ruby elastic-mapreduce --version
```

If the EMR CLI setup is correct and valid credentials are configured, these commands will display the EMR API version as output. You should see output similar to the following:

```
Version 2014-08-10
```

You can use the `--help` option to view the help information of the EMR CLI:

```
ruby elastic-mapreduce --help
```

Launching and monitoring an EMR cluster using CLI

Before launching an EMR cluster, you need to decide on the AWS region that will be used to launch the cluster and accordingly, you should have configured your `credentials.json` file. As discussed in our initial chapters, choosing a specific AWS region depends on factors such as your business location and latency requirements of connecting your existing data center or office with AWS using the virtual private network and so on for a secure data transfer.

Another important consideration is choosing the right instance type based on the analysis requirements. You would also need to consider an EMR cluster size depending on the size of data to be analyzed and stored in HDFS for processing. One m1.xlarge instance provides 1,680 GB of disk storage, so if you have an HDFS replication factor of 3, then you need at least three core nodes along with one master node for processing 1 TB of data. However, your cluster size also depends on the MapReduce job requirements for CPU and memory including the size of HDFS blocks and other factors. If you have a smaller cluster, then it could take longer to process the jobs and a large cluster with a smaller set of data would be a waste of money.

Since Hadoop can scale by adding more nodes, you can start with a smaller portion of data with a cluster to understand the job performance and tune the size of the cluster accordingly for the large data set. Let's say you have 100 GB of data to be processed, then you can work on 10 GB of that data and test your MapReduce jobs on a cluster size of three core nodes, which processes it in 1 hour. Then to process the 100 GB data in 1 hour, we would need 30 core nodes or use 10 core nodes to process it in 3 hours.

Launching an EMR cluster from command line

In *Chapter 6, Executing Hadoop Jobs on an Amazon EMR Cluster*, we executed our `HadoopHelloWorld` program on an EMR cluster from the AWS management console. We will now launch a similar cluster and execute the same MapReduce job from the command line. One point to note is that it will launch the machines in the region specified in the `credentials.json` file created earlier.

You can launch an EMR cluster with similar configuration, which we have used in the same chapter, using the following command:

```
ruby elastic-mapreduce --create --alive --name "HadoopHelloWorld
Test" \
--ami-version 3.0.4 \
--master-instance-type m1.medium --slave-instance-type m1.medium \
--num-instances 1 \
--bootstrap-action s3://elasticmapreduce/bootstrap-actions/install-
ganglia
```

If the cluster is successfully created, it should return the Job Flow ID of the cluster; the output would be something like the following:

```
Created job flow j-2LR6RDN91MJUI
```

This Job Flow ID will now be used to fetch information about the cluster, to add Job Steps, to check the status of the cluster as well as the added Job Steps, and also to terminate the cluster.

In the preceding command, the `--alive` option is used to keep the cluster in running state and not to terminate it until the `terminate cluster` command is issued from CLI or AWS EMR web console.

The `--ami-version` option is used to specify which EMR AMI provided by AWS is to be used for launching the Hadoop cluster. Since now the `--hadoop-version` parameter is not supported, `--ami-version` also determines the Hadoop version you want to install in your EMR cluster. We wanted to run on Hadoop 2.2.0; hence, we chose AMI Version 3.0.4. The following table shows the list of Hadoop versions along with the AMI version in which they are available.

Hadoop version	AMI version
2.4.0	3.1.0
2.2.0	3.0.4, 3.0.3, 3.0.2, and 3.0.1
1.0.3	2.4.5, 2.4.3, and 2.5.2
0.20.205	2.1.4
0.20	1.0

While launching a cluster, you can perform multiple other configurations, including overriding the region setting in the `credentials.json` file. The following is the list of all the available options you can use while creating a cluster using the CLI client:

- `--alive`: This is used in conjunction with `--create` to launch a cluster, which would continue running even after completing all the added Job Steps.

- `--ami-version <AMI_Version>`: This is used in conjunction with `--create` to launch a cluster with specific AMI version. This is also used to determine the Hadoop version in which your cluster is installed.

- `--availability-zone <Availability_Zone>`: This is used to specify the availability zone within the region where you want the machines forming the cluster to be launched.

- `--bootstrap-action <S3_Path> [--args "arg1,arg2"]`: This is used to provide any bootstrap action, which you might need to add to your cluster launch. In the preceding cluster launch command (`--create`), we added the install of Ganglia as part of our bootstrap action. You can refer *Chapter 7, Amazon EMR – Cluster Management*, for more details.

- `--bid-price <Bid_Price>`: This is used to specify the bid price in US dollars while using spot instances for your cluster. We will see how to launch a cluster using spot instances in a while.

- `--create`: This is used to create a cluster.

- `--instance-group INSTANCE_GROUP_TYPE`: This is used to set the instance group type. An instance group can be **MASTER**, **CORE**, or **TASK**.

- `--jobflow-role <IAM_Role_Name>`: This is used to launch the EC2 instances in the cluster with a specified IAM role.

- `--service-role <IAM_Role_Name>`: This is used to launch the Amazon EMR service with a specified IAM role.

- `--key-pair <Key_Pair_Pem_File>`: This is used to override the default key-pair information provided in the `credentials.json` file. If you want to use a specific key pair for your cluster, then you can use this option.

- `--master-instance-type <Instance_Type>`: This is used to specify the EC2 instance type to launch the master node.

- `--name "Cluster_Name"`: This is used to provide a name to the cluster.

- `--num-instances NUMBER_OF_INSTANCES`: This is used to specify the number of EC2 instances in the cluster. It is used in conjunction with either `--create` or `--modify-instance-group`.

- `--plain-output`: This is used when you want the output of a create cluster command to just return the `JobFlowID` value as plain text.

- `--region <Region>`: This is used to override the region setting in the `credentials.json` file.

- `--slave-instance-type`: This is used to specify the EC2 instance type to launch the slave nodes.

- `--subnet <EC2-Subnet_ID>`: This is used to launch the EMR cluster within an Amazon VPC subnet.

- `--visible-to-all-users <true|false>`: This can be used to make the instances in the cluster visible to all of your IAM users.

- `--with-supported-products <Product>`: This is used to install third-party software on the EMR cluster. It is used in conjunction with `--create`.

- `--with-termination-protection`: This is used to launch a cluster with **termination protection** enabled. It is used in conjunction with `--create`.

While testing your MapReduce jobs, you should launch the EMR cluster with the `--alive` option. Otherwise, when your job fails, even for a simple reason such as output location already exists, the cluster will terminate. When you are confident about your MapReduce code and have tested it a few times, then in production, you can let the cluster terminate as and when it completes the job, that is, do not use the `--alive` option then.

Adding Job Steps to the cluster

Now, after you have launched the cluster using the create cluster command as shown in the preceding section, you can use the following command to add the Job Step to execute our `HadoopHelloWorld` job of finding out hits by country:

```
ruby elastic-mapreduce --jobflow j-2LR6RDN91MJUI \
--jar s3://learning-bigdata/HadoopHelloWorld/bin/hits-by-country.jar
\
--args -D,"mapred.textoutputformat.separator=|" \
--args s3://learning-bigdata/HadoopHelloWorld/input/,s3://learning-
bigdata/HadoopHelloWorld/output/3/ \
--step-name "HadoopHelloWorld"
```

Note that the Job Flow ID to be used should be the same as that returned by the create cluster command. The `--jobflow` option is used to specify the Job Flow ID.

On successful addition of the Job Step, the following should output be returned:

```
Added jobflow steps
```

There are mainly three options while adding a Custom JAR Job Step:

- `--jar JAR_FILE_LOCATION [--args "arg1, arg2"]`: This is used to specify the path of the JAR file to be executed along with the arguments the JAR takes
- `--main-class`: This is used to specify the JAR's main class in case the JAR doesn't have a `manifest` file
- `--step-name`: This is used to provide a name to the Job Step.

You can also add streaming job steps using CLI. We will see how to execute streaming jobs in the next chapter.

Listing and getting details of EMR clusters

Now that you have added the Job Step using the command as shown in the preceding section, you can use the following command to view the list of active clusters along with their Job Steps:

```
ruby elastic-mapreduce --list --active
```

This command will return with the following list of clusters:

```
j-2LR6RDN91MJUI     BOOTSTRAPPING  ec2-54-87-166-19.compute-
1.amazonaws.com     HadoopHelloWorld Test

PENDING             HadoopHelloWorld
```

If you want to just list the clusters without the steps, then use the `--no-steps` option as shown here:

```
ruby elastic-mapreduce --list --active --no-steps
```

You can review the details of recent clusters launched during the last 2 days using the following command:

```
ruby elastic-mapreduce --list
```

This command's output will show the recent clusters including their Job Flow ID, status, name, and the list of the Job Steps along with their statuses as well.

Using the `--active` option along with `--list` will show only active clusters in the output. Also, using the `--state` option, you can view the clusters in specific statuses such as **RUNNING**, **STARTING**, **SHUTTING_DOWN**, and **BOOTSTRAPPING**, among others.

To view the job flow details of a specific cluster, you can use the following command:

```
ruby elastic-mapreduce --describe --jobflow <JobFlowID>
```

In our case, we will execute the following command to get the details of our cluster:

```
ruby elastic-mapreduce --describe --jobflow j-2LR6RDN91MJUI
```

The output of this command is as follows:

```
{
  "JobFlows": [
    {
      "BootstrapActions": [
        {
          "BootstrapActionConfig": {
```

```
          "Name": "Bootstrap Action 1",
          "ScriptBootstrapAction": {
            "Path": "s3:\/\/elasticmapreduce\/bootstrap-
            actions\/install-ganglia",
            "Args": []
          }
        }
      }
    }
  ],
  "Name": "HadoopHelloWorld Test",
  "Instances": {
    "InstanceGroups": [
      {
        "ReadyDateTime": 1406436263.304,
        "InstanceType": "m1.medium",
        "Name": "Master Instance Group",
        "CreationDateTime": 1406435906.265,
        "State": "ENDED",
        "InstanceGroupId": "ig-F7ELQBAQRN9U",
        "StartDateTime": 1406436263.304,
        "InstanceRole": "MASTER",
        "Market": "ON_DEMAND",
        "LastStateChangeReason": "Job flow terminated",
        "EndDateTime": 1406437150.709,
        "InstanceRunningCount": 0,
        "InstanceRequestCount": 1
      }
    ],
    "InstanceCount": 1,
    "MasterInstanceType": "m1.medium",
    "MasterPublicDnsName": "ec2-54-87-166-19.compute-
    1.amazonaws.com",
    "KeepJobFlowAliveWhenNoSteps": true,
    "Ec2KeyName": "learning-bigdata",
    "TerminationProtected": false,
    "NormalizedInstanceHours": 2,
```

```
    "HadoopVersion": "2.2.0",
    "Placement": {
      "AvailabilityZone": "us-east-1b"
    },
    "MasterInstanceId": "i-40aef86c"
  },
  "ExecutionStatusDetail": {
    "ReadyDateTime": 1406436268.108,
    "CreationDateTime": 1406435906.264,
    "State": "TERMINATED",
    "StartDateTime": 1406436127.987,
    "LastStateChangeReason": "Terminated by user request",
    "EndDateTime": 1406437151.122
  },
  "AmiVersion": "3.0.4",
  "VisibleToAllUsers": false,
  "JobFlowId": "j-2LR6RDN91MJUI",
  "SupportedProducts": [],
  "Steps": [
    {
      "StepConfig": {
        "ActionOnFailure": "CANCEL_AND_WAIT",
        "Name": "HadoopHelloWorld",
        "HadoopJarStep": {
          "Properties": [],
          "Jar": "s3:\/\/learning-
          bigdata\/HadoopHelloWorld\/bin\/hits-by-country.jar",
          "Args": [
            "-D",
            "mapred.textoutputformat.separator=|",
            "s3:\/\/learning-bigdata\/HadoopHelloWorld\/input\/",
            "s3:\/\/learning-
            bigdata\/HadoopHelloWorld\/output\/3\/"
          ]
        }
      },
```

```
        "ExecutionStatusDetail": {
          "CreationDateTime": 1406436701.295,
          "State": "COMPLETED",
          "StartDateTime": 1406436707.372,
          "EndDateTime": 1406436809.41
        }
      }
    ],
    "LogUri": "s3n:\/\/learning-bigdata\/emr-logs\/"
  }
  ]
}
```

Terminating an EMR cluster

When your Job Step has completed you would want to terminate the cluster. In order to find out whether your Job Step has completed or not, you can execute the `list` command as follows:

```
ruby elastic-mapreduce --list --active
j-2LR6RDN91MJUI       WAITING          ec2-54-87-166-19.compute-
1.amazonaws.com           HadoopHelloWorld Test
   COMPLETED      HadoopHelloWorld
```

If the status of your Job Step is **COMPLETED**, then you can now go ahead and terminate the cluster. If it has failed, then you can check out the logs and figure out the reason, correct it, add the Job Step again, and wait for it to complete.

We can terminate an existing cluster using the EMR CLI command as follows:

```
ruby elastic-mapreduce --terminate <JobFlowID>
```

In our case, we will execute the following command to terminate the cluster launched in the earlier section:

```
ruby elastic-mapreduce --terminate j-2LR6RDN91MJUI
```

On successful termination, this will return with the following output:

```
Terminated job flow j-2LR6RDN91MJUI
```

Using spot instances with EMR

AWS states the following:

> *"Spot Instances allow you to name your own price for Amazon EC2 computing capacity. You simply bid on spare Amazon EC2 instances and run them whenever your bid exceeds the current Spot Price, which varies in real-time based on supply and demand."*

Using spot instances can certainly prove very cost effective but it is prudent to use spot instances only for time-flexible and interruption-tolerant tasks. As and when the current spot price goes above your bidding price, the instance can be taken away from you, though you will not be charged for that hour in which it was taken away. The MapReduce jobs aren't generally interruption tolerant; hence, in order to use spot instances while still not losing our cluster, we need to use a balance of on-demand and spot instances.

As discussed earlier in *Chapter 4, Amazon EMR – Hadoop on Amazon Web Services*, we have three different types of nodes and hence, three instance groups can be formed:

- **Master instance group**: This consists of only a single master instance
- **Core instance group**: This consists of those instances that would execute our Job Steps as well as provide storage for HDFS
- **Task instance group**: This consists of those instances that will only execute our Job Steps

You can choose to run spot instances for all the mentioned instance groups, but it is not recommended to have a master instance procured as a spot instance. Similarly, even with instances in the core instance group, it is not advised to use spot instances because you might lose data.

Hence, the best and most safe way to use spot instances is to have a percentage of total instances in your cluster launched as on-demand and as part of the core instance group and the rest as spot instances and as part of the task instance group.

For example, if you want to launch a cluster with 10 m1.xlarge slave nodes and an m1.medium master node and you also want to use spot instances, you can use the following command to launch the instance from CLI:

```
ruby elastic-mapreduce --create --alive --name "Cluster Using Spot" \
--ami-version 3.0.4 \
--instance-group master –instance-type m1.medium –instance-count 1 \
--instance-group core –instance-type m1.xlarge –instance-count 4 \
```

```
--instance-group task -instance-type m1.xlarge -instance-count 6 --
bid-price 0.20 \
```

```
--bootstrap-action s3://elasticmapreduce/bootstrap-actions/install-
ganglia
```

If you see, we have divided the total number of slave nodes among the core and task groups. This division depends on how much data you are going to store in HDFS. If it is going to be considerable, then you can increase the number of nodes in the core group. Also, having a very low number of nodes in the core group will result in too many network calls in reading data by the instances in the task group.

Summary

In this chapter, you learned to install and use the EMR Ruby client to launch a cluster, add steps to it, and terminate the cluster when the steps are completed. We also saw how to use spot instances with EMR.

In the next chapter, you will learn how to execute streaming jobs from CLI. We will also see some advanced concepts such as implementing custom partitioner and multiple outputs.

9
Hadoop Streaming and Advanced Hadoop Customizations

In this chapter, we will learn how to use scripting languages such as Python or Ruby to create mappers and reducers instead of using Java. We will see how to launch a streaming EMR cluster and also how to add a streaming Job Step to an already running cluster. We will also see some advanced concepts such as implementing custom partitioner and emitting results to multiple outputs.

Hadoop streaming

This is basically a prebuilt utility that comes along with the Hadoop distribution. It allows you to create a MapReduce job using any executable program or script as the mapper and reducer.

As discussed in *Chapter 5*, *Programming Hadoop on Amazon EMR*, let's say you have your local copy of Hadoop distribution in `<hadoop-2.2.0-base-path>`. You should be able to find the streaming utility jar file in `<hadoop-2.2.0-base-path>/share/hadoop/tools/lib/hadoop-streaming-2.2.0.jar`. Say you have written your mapper and reducer in Python, and you have `mapper.py` and `reducer.py` as your mapper and reducer respectively. Now, locally you can use the streaming utility by executing the following command:

```
<hadoop-2.2.0-base-path>/bin/hadoop  jar <hadoop-2.2.0-base-
path>/share/hadoop/tools/lib/hadoop-streaming-2.2.0.jar \
    -input <inputDirectoryOrFile> \
    -output <outputDirectory> \
    -mapper mapper.py \
    -reducer reducer.py
```

How streaming works

The executables should be created in such a way that they read input from STDIN and emit output to STDOUT. The input is read line by line by default.

Each mapper task will launch the executable as a separate process when it is initialized. Now, the streaming utility reads the input provided with the streaming job and passes on to the executable. It reads the input line by line and feeds the lines to STDIN of the mapper executable process. The output from the mapper executable is also expected to be line based and is expected to be written to STDOUT. Now, it's the job of the streaming utility to convert each line into a key-value pair.

Each reducer task also works in the same manner.

> By default, the tab character is considered to be the separator between the key and the value. So, the part of a line up to the first tab character is the key and the rest of the line (excluding the tab character) will be the value. If there is no tab character in the line, then the entire line is considered as the key and the value is null. However, you can customize this; we will see how to do this in a later section.

Wordcount example with streaming

In order to demonstrate what was explained in the preceding section, let's create the mapper and reducer in Python for a simple task of counting words in the given input.

Mapper

Inside the mapper.py file, you would loop into sys.stdin as the streaming utility will bring all the input line by line to the executable's standard input (STDIN).

You can then split the line into words and for each word emit a count of 1, which can then be aggregated in the reducer to get the count of each word.

Your mapper.py file's content will look as follows:

```
#!/usr/bin/python

import sys

# In hadoop streaming, the input files are read and provided to
mapper as input from STDIN
```

```
for line in sys.stdin:

    # trim the input line of any whitespaces
    line = line.strip()
    results = line.split()
    for word in results:
        # emitting the tab-delimited result to STDOUT
        print '%s\t%s' % (word, 1)
```

Reducer

Inside the reducer.py file, you would again loop into sys.stdin as the streaming utility will bring all the output from mapper line by line to the executable reducer's standard input (STDIN).

Here, you are not going to get all the values for a given key together as we get in custom JAR implementation. However, the following two factors make it easy to write logic in the reducer:

- The input received by reducer is sorted
- All data related to a given key will reach a single reducer

Hence, in your reducer, you can get a count for the key until the key changes. The following content of reducer.py will explain it:

```
#!/usr/bin/python

import sys

key = None
currentKey = None
currentCount = 0

# In hadoop streaming, the output from mapper is received by reducer
as input from STDIN
for line in sys.stdin:

    # trim the input line of any whitespaces
    line = line.strip()

    key, count = line.split('\t', 1)

    try:
        count = int(count)
```

```
    except ValueError:
        continue

    # Since all the keys are sorted before it is passed to the
reducer,
    # we can count till we find a different key
    if currentKey == key:
        currentCount += count
    else:
        if currentKey:
            # Results are emitted to STDOUT
            print '%s,%s' % (currentKey, currentCount)
        currentCount = count
        currentKey = key

# This section makes sure that the last key is also emitted
if currentKey == key:
    print '%s,%s' % (currentKey, currentCount)
```

If you noticed, here we are not emitting output as tab delimited; hence, the entire line emitted to STDOUT becomes the key and the value is empty. However, since the utility considers the tab character as the default separator, each of the lines in our final output from the reducer will have a tab character at the end as the value is empty.

Streaming command options

The streaming utility supports a list of options. It also supports generic command options.

The general command-line syntax is as follows:

```
bin/hadoop command [genericOptions] [streamingOptions]
```

 The generic options should be placed before the streaming options, otherwise the streaming job will fail.

The following section provides a list of options that the streaming utility supports.

Mandatory parameters

The following are the mandatory parameters:

Parameter	Description
-input <inputDirectoryOrFile>	Input location to a directory or a file
-output <directory>	Output directory location; this location should not already exist
-mapper <executableOrJavaClassName>	Path to the mapper executable or a Java class name
-reducer <executableOrJavaClassName>	Path to the reducer executable or a Java class name

 Multiple input directories with multiple -input options:

```
hadoop jar hadoop-streaming.jar -input /inputs/dir1
-input  /inputs/dir2
```

Optional parameters

The following are the optional parameters:

Parameter	Description
-file <fileName>	Makes the mapper, reducer, or combiner executable available locally on the compute nodes.
-inputFormat <javaClassName>	The class you supply should return key/value pairs of the Text class. If not specified, TextInputFormat is used as the default.
-outputFormat <javaClassName>	The Class you supply should take key/value pairs of the Text class. If not specified, TextOutputformat is used as the default.
-partitioner <javaClassName>	Class that determines which reducer task a key is sent to.
-combiner <executableOrJavaClassName>	Path to the combiner executable or a Java class name.
-cmdenv <name=value>	Pass an environment variable to streaming commands.
-verbose	Provides verbose output.

Parameter	Description
-lazyOutput	Creates output lazily. For example, if the output format is based on FileOutputFormat, the output file is created only on the first call to output.collect (or Context.write)
-numReduceTasks	Specifies the number of reducers.
-mapdebug	Path to a script which will be called when a map task fails.
-reducedebug	Path to a script which will be called when a reduce task fails.

Using a Java class name as mapper/reducer

As you have seen from the preceding options, you can specify a Java class as mapper and/or reducer for your streaming job. Hadoop has some prebuilt classes that can be used for general use cases.

For example, if your task is to just sum up each user's time spent on your website for the full year, your input will be something like the following:

```
Day1,user1,11234
Day1,user2,1098
. . .
DayN,user1,2008
DayN,user2,456
```

In this case, you would not want to do anything in the mapper and hence, you can use the prebuilt org.apache.hadoop.mapred.lib.IdentityMapper class as your mapper. Its usage will be as follows:

```
<hadoop-2.2.0-base-path>/bin/hadoop  jar <hadoop-2.2.0-base-path>/share/hadoop/tools/lib/hadoop-streaming-2.2.0.jar \
    -input <inputDirectoryOrFile> \
    -output <outputDirectory> \
    -mapper org.apache.hadoop.mapred.lib.IdentityMapper \
    -reducer reducer.py
```

Using generic command options with streaming

You can use generic options with streaming the same way you would use them with custom JAR execution. Care should be taken that the generic options should be provided before the streaming options.

You can specify configuration variables using the -D option. You can also provide the list of files, jars, or archives to be copied to the Map/Reduce cluster. The following is a list of important generic options supported with streaming:

Parameter	Description
-conf <configurationFile>	Path to an application configuration file
-D <property=value>	Specifies Hadoop/MapReduce configuration variables
-files <commaSeparatedList>	Provides comma-separated files to be copied to the Map/Reduce cluster
-libjars <commaSeparatedList>	Provides comma-separated jar files to include in the class path
-archives <commaSeparatedList>	Provides comma-separated archives to be unarchived on the compute machines

For example, if you want to set a number of reducers while executing your streaming job, you can execute the following command:

```
<hadoop-2.2.0-base-path>/bin/hadoop  jar <hadoop-2.2.0-base-
path>/share/hadoop/tools/lib/hadoop-streaming-2.2.0.jar \
    -D mapred.reduce.tasks=2 \
    -input <inputDirectoryOrFile> \
    -output <outputDirectory> \
    -mapper mapper.py \
    -reducer reducer.py
```

Customizing key-value splitting

As discussed earlier, the streaming utility reads the input line by line and each line is split into a key and value pair considering that, by default, the separator is a tab character. So, everything in a line before the first occurrence of a tab character is considered as key and everything after the first tab character is considered as value.

You can customize both the following aspects of a line being split into key value:

- The separator character. This can be done using the following configuration parameters:
  - ° `stream.map.input.field.separator`
  - ° `stream.map.output.field.separator`
  - ° `stream.reduce.input.field.separator`
  - ° `stream.reduce.output.field.separator`

- The occurrence number of the character to be taken as separation (instead of default first occurrence). This can be done using the following configuration parameters:
  - ° `stream.num.map.input.key.fields`
  - ° `stream.num.map.output.key.fields`
  - ° `stream.num.reduce.input.key.fields`
  - ° `stream.num.reduce.output.key.fields`

So, let's say that you want to split the output line from the mapper into key and value using the hyphen character and you want the first occurrence of the hyphen to remain as part of the key and split from the second occurrence, you can use the following command:

```
<hadoop-2.2.0-base-path>/bin/hadoop  jar <hadoop-2.2.0-base-
path>/share/hadoop/tools/lib/hadoop-streaming-2.2.0.jar \
    -D stream.map.output.field.separator=- \
    -D stream.num.map.output.key.fields=2 \
    -D mapred.reduce.tasks=2 \
    -input <inputDirectoryOrFile> \
    -output <outputDirectory> \
    -mapper mapper.py \
    -reducer reducer.py
```

Hence, consider one of your mapper output lines has the following data:

```
key-1-value-1
```

Using the mentioned configurations, this line will be split as follows:

```
key = key-1
value = value-1
```

Using Hadoop partitioner class

You might need to partition the map outputs based on certain parts of the key rather than the whole key. Hadoop already has a library class that allows you to decide what proportion of the key should be used in partitioning mapper output data among reducers. The useful class is `org.apache.hadoop.mapreduce.lib.partition.KeyFieldBasedPartitioner`.

You can use it as shown in the following command:

```
<hadoop-2.2.0-base-path>/bin/hadoop  jar <hadoop-2.2.0-base-path>/share/hadoop/tools/lib/hadoop-streaming-2.2.0.jar \
    -D stream.map.output.field.separator=- \
    -D stream.num.map.output.key.fields=2 \
    -D map.output.key.field.separator=- \
    -D mapred.text.key.partitioner.options=-k1 \
    -D mapred.reduce.tasks=2 \
    -input <inputDirectoryOrFile> \
    -output <outputDirectory> \
    -mapper mapper.py \
    -reducer reducer.py
    -partitioner
    org.apache.hadoop.mapred.lib.KeyFieldBasedPartitioner
```

You might notice the following two new configuration parameters in this command:

- `map.output.key.field.separator`: This specifies the character on which the key will be separated into fields.

- `mapred.text.key.partitioner.options`: This specifies all the fields from which the key has to be considered for partitioning. Its value is specified in the form `-k position1[,position2]`.

Say, we get the following mapper outputs:

```
keyOne-100-value-1
keyTwo-8-value-3
keyAnother-21-valueAnother-1
keyOne-3-value-2
keyAnother-2-valueAnother-2
```

Since we have set `stream.map.output.field.separator` as hyphen (-) and `stream.num.map.output.key.fields` as 2, we have the following list of keys ready to be partitioned among reducers:

`keyOne-100`

`keyTwo-8`

`keyAnother-21`

`keyOne-3`

`keyAnother-2`

Now, since we have set `map.output.key.field.separator` as hyphen and `mapred.text.key.partitioner.options` as `-k1`, this means that we are separating our key into fields using the hyphen character and want to partition them only on the basis of first field among them.

Hence, we have the mentioned keys partitioned into three reducers as follows:

- For `Reducer1`, we have the following keys::
    - `keyOne-100`
    - `keyOne-3`

- For `Reducer2`, we have the following key:
    - `keyTwo-8`

- For `Reducer3`, we have the following keys:
    - `keyAnother-21`
    - `keyAnother-2`

Sorting of keys happens within each partition and all the fields will be used for sorting; hence, the reducers will receive input in the following order:

- For `Reducer1`, the input is:
    - **`keyOne-3`**
    - `keyOne-100`

- For `Reducer2`, the input is:
    - `keyTwo-8`

- For `Reducer3`, the input is:
    - `keyAnother-2`
    - `keyAnother-21`

In our last section, we will see how we can create our own custom partitioner in Java.

Using Hadoop comparator class

Hadoop already has a library class that allows you to decide which parts of the mapper output keys should be used in sorting before passing on the data to the reducers. The useful class is `org.apache.hadoop.mapreduce.lib.partition.` `KeyFieldBasedComparator`.

You can use it as shown in the following command:

```
<hadoop-2.2.0-base-path>/bin/hadoop  jar <hadoop-2.2.0-base-
path>/share/hadoop/tools/lib/hadoop-streaming-2.2.0.jar \
    -D mapred.output.key.comparator.class=org.apache.hadoop.mapred.lib.
KeyFieldBasedComparator \
    -D stream.map.output.field.separator=- \
    -D stream.num.map.output.key.fields=2 \
    -D map.output.key.field.separator=- \
    -D mapred.text.key.partitioner.options=-k1 \
    -D mapred.text.key.comparator.options=-k2,2nr \
    -D mapred.reduce.tasks=2 \
    -input <inputDirectoryOrFile> \
    -output <outputDirectory> \
    -mapper mapper.py \
    -reducer reducer.py \
    -partitioner
    org.apache.hadoop.mapred.lib.KeyFieldBasedPartitioner
```

Here, in this command, we are forced to use the first field of the key for partitioning while using the second field for sorting. Using -n indicates numerical sorting while using -r indicates reverse sorting, that is, sorting in descending order; hence, the reducers will receive input in the following order:

- For `Reducer1`, the input will be received as:
    ◦ keyOne-100
    ◦ keyOne-3

- For `Reducer2`, the input will be received as:
    ◦ keyTwo-8

- For `Reducer3`, the input will be received as:
    ◦ keyAnother-21
    ◦ keyAnother-2

In our last section, we will see how we can create our own custom comparator class in Java.

Adding streaming Job Step on EMR

Now, let's see how you can execute a streaming job on an EMR cluster. You can refer to *Chapter 6, Executing Hadoop Jobs on an Amazon EMR Cluster*, to launch an EMR cluster from the AWS management console and you can refer to *Chapter 8, Amazon EMR – Command-line Interface Client*, to launch a cluster using the CLI client tool.

Using the AWS management console

While you are launching the cluster in the **Steps** section, select **Streaming program** from the **Add step** drop-down selection, as shown in the following screenshot:

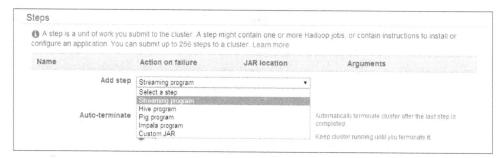

After that, click on **Configure and add**. This will bring up a pop-up box where you can define various parameters for your streaming job. You should have your mapper and reducer executables along with the input files to be present in S3. The following screenshot shows the various parameters:

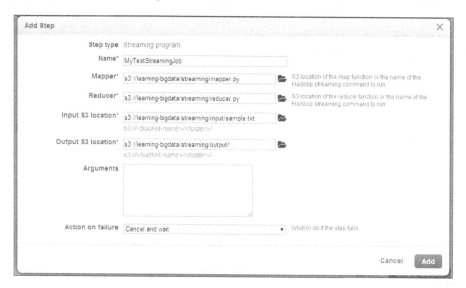

After you have entered the required parameters, click on **Add**. Optionally, you can also enter a list of arguments (space-separated strings) to pass to the Hadoop streaming utility. For example, you can specify additional files to be copied to the cluster using the `-files` option.

Continue with other cluster configurations and then launch the cluster. Your streaming job should get executed along with the other added Job Steps.

Using the CLI client

Assuming that you have already launched a cluster using CLI as explained in *Chapter 8*, *Amazon EMR – Command-line Interface Client*, and you have the `jobFlowId` value for the cluster with you, you can add a streaming Job Step by executing the following command:

```
ruby elastic-mapreduce -j <jobFlowId> --stream    \
--args "-files,s3://learning-bigdata/streaming/mapper.py" \
--step-name "MyTestStreamingJob" \
--jobconf mapreduce.job.reduces=2 \
--mapper mapper.py \
--reducer s3://learning-bigdata/streaming/reducer.py \
--input s3://learning-bigdata/streaming/input/sample.txt \
--output s3://learning-bigdata/streaming/output
```

In this command, you will notice that we have specified the number of reducers by using the `--jobconf` option.

 If you are using earlier versions of Hadoop instead of `mapreduce.job.reduces`, you would use `mapred.reduce.tasks` to set the number of reducers for your Job Step.

You might also have noticed that for the `mapper` option, we have just provided the `mapper.py` executable name instead of the full S3 path. This is just to demonstrate that you can use the `--args` option to pass on other Hadoop streaming options such as `-files`, which in the case of the preceding command will copy the `mapper.py` file from the specified S3 location to each node in the cluster, making the `mapper.py` file locally available to all the map tasks.

Launching a streaming cluster using the CLI client

Instead of first launching a cluster and then adding the streaming Job Step to it, you can also launch a streaming cluster.

As we have seen in *Chapter 8, Amazon EMR – Command-line Interface Client*, if you want to launch a cluster with specific versions, you should use the `ami-version` option; also, for Hadoop 2.x, only machine types with configurations higher than or equal to m1.medium are allowed. Keeping these two things in mind, you can launch a streaming cluster by executing the following command:

```
ruby elastic-mapreduce --create --stream --ami-version 3.0.3 \
--instance-type m1.medium --instance-count 1 \
--args "-files,s3://learning-bigdata/streaming/mapper.py" \
--name "MyTestStreamingJob" \
--jobconf mapreduce.job.reduces=2 \
--mapper mapper.py \
--reducer s3://learning-bigdata/streaming/reducer.py \
--input s3://learning-bigdata/streaming/input/sample.txt \
--output s3://learning-bigdata/streaming/output
```

If you do not provide the `instance-count` option, by default, a cluster with a single node will be created.

Advanced Hadoop customizations

When you are creating the custom JAR implementation for a Hadoop job, you have the flexibility to customize most of the default implementations being used. You can create your own implementation of `InputFormat` and `OutputFormat`, and you can create your own key and value classes to be used in place of `LongWritable` or `Text` classes. You can also customize the way your Map/Reduce job will partition and sort data. You have already seen how to create custom counters in *Chapter 5, Programming Hadoop on Amazon EMR*.

In this section, we will see how to create your own implementation of a partitioner and a sorting comparator.

Custom partitioner

You can create your own implementation of partitioner by extending org.apache. hadoop.mapreduce.Partitioner. The following is the implementation of a partitioner performing function similar to the one in the previous section:

```
import org.apache.hadoop.io.Text;
import org.apache.hadoop.mapreduce.Partitioner;
import org.apache.hadoop.mapreduce.lib.partition.HashPartitioner;

public class KeyFieldsPartitioner extends Partitioner<Text, Text> {

    HashPartitioner<Text, Text> hashPartitioner =
        new HashPartitioner<Text, Text>();
    Text newKey = new Text();

    @Override
    public int getPartition(Text key, Text value, int
        numReduceTasks) {

        try {

            // Get the first field of the key
            String keyString = key.toString();
            String[] keyFields = keyString.split("-");
            newKey.set(keyFields[0]);

            // Execute the default partitioner over the first
                    field of the key
            return hashPartitioner.getPartition(newKey, value,
                    numReduceTasks);
        } catch (Exception e) {
            e.printStackTrace();
            return (int) (Math.random() * numReduceTasks);
                    // this would return a random value in the range
                            // [0,numReduceTasks)
        }
    }
}
```

So, basically, here you need to extend the Partitioner class and override its getPartition method. This method should return an integer in the range [0, numReduceTasks).

Within this method's implementation, the key is split into fields using a hyphen (-) as the separator and then the partition is decided only on the basis of the first field. We are executing the default HashPartitioner over the first field.

Using a custom partitioner

In order to instruct your Map/Reduce job to use your custom implementation of the partitioner, you need to use the setPartitionerClass method of the org.apache.hadoop.mapreduce.Job class.

So, if you refer to the Driver implementation in *Chapter 5, Programming Hadoop on Amazon EMR*, you can add the following line in the overridden run method:

```
Configuration conf = getConf();
Job job = Job.getInstance(conf);
...

job.setPartitionerClass(KeyFieldsPartitioner.class);

...
boolean success = job.waitForCompletion(true);
return success ? 0 : 1;
```

Custom sort comparator

Similar to creating the custom partitioner, you can create your own implementation of a sort comparator by extending the org.apache.hadoop.io.WritableComparator class and overriding the compare method. The following is the implementation of a sort comparator performing function similar to the one in the previous section:

```
import org.apache.hadoop.io.Text;
import org.apache.hadoop.io.WritableComparable;
import org.apache.hadoop.io.WritableComparator;

public class KeyFieldsComparator extends WritableComparator {
    protected KeyFieldsComparator() {
        super(Text.class, true);
    }
    @SuppressWarnings("rawtypes")
    @Override
    public int compare(WritableComparable w1, WritableComparable
    w2) {
```

```
        Text key1 = (Text) w1;
        Text key2 = (Text) w2;

        // Get the fields of the key
        String keyString1 = key1.toString();
        String[] keyFields1 = keyString1.split("-");

        String keyString2 = key2.toString();
        String[] keyFields2 = keyString2.split("-");

        // (compare on the second part of the key)
        int compare = keyFields1[1].compareTo(keyFields2[1]);

        return compare;
    }
}
```

If you see, we are comparing keys on the basis of the second field after splitting the key using the hyphen (-) character.

The preceding comparator implementation sorts in ascending order; if you want to sort in reverse order, then you just need to reverse the comparison section, as follows:

```
        int compare = keyFields2[1].compareTo(keyFields1[1]);
```

Using custom sort comparator

In order to instruct your Map/Reduce job to use your custom implementation of the sort comparator, you need to use the setSortComparatorClass method of the org.apache.hadoop.mapreduce.Job class.

If you refer to the driver implementation in *Chapter 5, Programming Hadoop on Amazon EMR*, you can add the following line in the overridden run method:

```
        Configuration conf = getConf();
        Job job = Job.getInstance(conf);
        ...

        job.setSortComparatorClass(KeyFieldsComparator.class);

        ...
        boolean success = job.waitForCompletion(true);
        return success ? 0 : 1;
```

Emitting results to multiple outputs

Hadoop provides a utility class `org.apache.hadoop.mapreduce.lib.output.MultipleOutputs` that simplifies writing output data to multiple files and locations.

You might use `MultipleOutputs` mainly for the following two use cases:

- To emit additional outputs other than the job default output
- To emit data to different files and/or directories provided by a user

Using MultipleOutputs

Each additional output or named output might be configured with its own output format, key class, and value class. You can define multiple named outputs in your `Driver` class and then use them in your `Reducer` class to emit additional output. Each `Reducer` class creates a separate copy of these named outputs, the same way it does with default job output.

Usage in the Driver class

You can use the following static method of the `MutilpleOutputs` class to define a named output, which will be in addition to the job default output:

```
addNamedOutput(Job job, String namedOutput, Class<? extends
OutputFormat> outputFormatClass, Class<?> keyClass, Class<?>
valueClass)
```

So, if you refer to the `Driver` implementation in *Chapter 5, Programming Hadoop on Amazon EMR*, you can add the following line in the overridden `run` method:

```
Configuration conf = getConf();
Job job = Job.getInstance(conf);
...


// Defines additional single text based output 'text' for the job
 MultipleOutputs.addNamedOutput(job, "text", TextOutputFormat.class,
 LongWritable.class, Text.class);


...
boolean success = job.waitForCompletion(true);
return success ? 0 : 1;
```

This code will let you emit some additional data into an additional set of output files from each `Reducer` class; hence, with the usual `part-r-00000`, `part-00001` and so on, you can also see output files named `text-00000`, `text-00001` and so on in your output directory.

Usage in the Reducer class

After defining the named outputs in the `Driver` class, you can use them in your `Reducer` class to emit additional output data.

Within your `Reducer` class, you should create an instance of the `MultipleOutputs` class in the `setup` method, as shown here:

```
private MultipleOutputs multipleOutputsInstance;
public void setup(Context context) {
    ...
    multipleOutputsInstance = new MultipleOutputs(context);
}
```

Now, within the reduce method implementation, you can use the `write` method of the `MultipleOutputs` class to emit output. The following three variants of the `write` method are available:

- `write(String namedOutput, K key, V value)`: This is the `write` key and value to `namedOutput`. You can use it in your reduce method implementation as follows:

  ```
  multipleOutputsInstance.write("text", key, new
    Text("Hello"));
  ```

- `write(String namedOutput, K key, V value, String baseOutputPath)`: This is the `write` key and value to `baseOutputPath` using `namedOutput`. The only difference this method has from the first one is that it allows you to emit additional outputs to more than one file for the same named output, that is, you can provide different `baseOutputPaths`; however, the framework will generate a unique filename for `baseOutputPath`. The `/` characters in `baseOutputPath` will be translated into directory levels in your filesystem. You can use it in your reduce method implementation as follows:

  ```
  multipleOutputsInstance.write("text", key, new
    Text("Hello"),"output/1"); .
  multipleOutputsInstance.write("text", key, new
    Text("Hello"),"output/2");
  ```

- `write(KEYOUT key, VALUEOUT value, String baseOutputPath)`: This is the `write` key value to an output filename. When you use it, make sure that the job's output format should be a `FileOutputFormat`. You can use it in your reduce method implementation as follows:

    ```
    multipleOutputsInstance.write(key, new Text("Hello"),"output/1");
    ```

Do not forget to close the `multipleOutputsInstance`. The best place to do this is the `cleanup` method:

```
public void cleanup(Context) throws IOException {
    multipleOutputsInstance.close();
    ...
}
```

Emitting outputs in different directories based on key and value

Often, you might want to segregate outputs depending on some key or value data. You can create a method that accepts both key and value and emits a relative file path and uses that in conjunction with the last variant of the `write` method, as shown in the previous section.

For example, your key has both `Country` and `City` separated with a hyphen and you want each country's data to be emitted in separate directories. Also, the filenames will have names starting with the city name. You can achieve this by following this short method:

```
private String generateFileName(Text key) {
    // "Country-City"
    String[] keyParts = key.toString().split("-");

    String country = keyParts [0];
    String city = keyParts [1];
    return country + "/" + city;
}
```

Also in your `reduce` method, you can emit the output as follows:

```
multipleOutputsInstance.write(key, value, generateFileName(key));
```

Now, say your key was `India-Bangalore` and the output directory for your job is `/user/learning-bigdata/output/`, the output from the first reducer would be written to `/user/learning-bigdata/output/India/Bangalore-r-00000`.

To achieve this, adding any named output is not required in your `Driver` class. Also, no call to `context.write()` is necessary in your `reduce` method implementation if you just want to emit your output via `MultipleOutputs` into different locations. But using `MultipleOutputs` in this way will still create zero-sized default output files (`part-00000`). In order to prevent this, you can use the `org.apache.hadoop.mapreduce.lib.output.LazyOutputFormat` class.

You just need to change the way you define your `OutputFormat` class in your `Driver` implementation.

In your `OutputFormat` class, consider the following code:

```
job.setOutputFormatClass(TextOutputFormat.class);
```

Instead of the preceding code, you can use the following:

```
LazyOutputFormat.setOutputFormatClass(job, TextOutputFormat.class)
```

This code delays the creation of the output file until any data is available to be written, and while you use `MultipleOutputs` exclusively instead of `context.write()` to emit your output, you would certainly not want the empty part files to be created.

Summary

In this chapter, we learned about Hadoop streaming and how it works. We also saw how to run streaming jobs on Amazon EMR. We learned how to create custom partitioners and custom comparators in Java, and we also saw how to emit output from a Hadoop job in multiple files and directories.

In the next chapter, we will build upon the sample Hadoop solution that we created in *Chapter 5, Programming Hadoop on Amazon EMR*.

10
Use Case – Analyzing CloudFront Logs Using Amazon EMR

In this chapter, we will use all that we learned in previous chapters to build a real solution to analyze Amazon CloudFront logs using Hadoop and then use a visualization tool to show that data in a tabular and/or graphical format.

Use case definition

As we have seen in our first chapter, Amazon CloudFront is a content delivery web service that helps end users to distribute content with low-latency to their customers. Amazon CloudFront uses its edge locations that are spread across the world to deliver content. Requests originating from any place are served by the nearest edge location resulting in the desired low latency.

Now, say you are using Amazon CloudFront as the CDN service for your website and you want to know the access trends across the world for your website. Basically, you want to get the total request count, hit count, miss count, error count, per city per country. You want to be able to see how many bytes have been transferred per edge location. You also want to get the breakdown of all the requests on the basis of HTTP status codes. That is, for example, how many 404 errors were there.

So, our use case here is to get insights from Amazon CloudFront access logs analysis.

The solution architecture

When you create an Amazon CloudFront distribution, you can enable access logging. When enabled, Amazon CloudFront saves the access logs in a W3C extended format into a S3 bucket that you define.

The following diagram depicts the solution architecture:

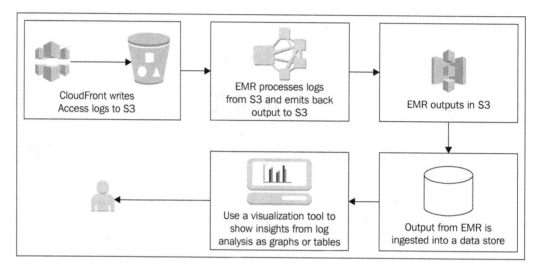

So, we will use Hadoop to do the parsing, IP to city/country mapping, and aggregation among other things.

Amazon EMR will be used to execute this Hadoop Job Step and emit the results into an output S3 bucket.

The output of our Hadoop Job Step will be ingested into a data store; for this solution, we will use MySQL as our data store, but you can choose more distributed and scalable data stores such as Amazon Redshift if you are actually moving this solution to production, depending on the volume and velocity of your CloudFront logs.

For creating graphs and charts, we will use a visualization tool named Tableau; you can also use other tools such as Jaspersoft as well.

Creating the Hadoop Job Step

You need to build on to the `Hello World` example we saw in *Chapter 5, Programming Hadoop on Amazon EMR.*

Inputs and required libraries

Let's first understand what inputs are available to us and what more metadata we need.

This Hadoop Job Step will take the following data as input:

- CloudFront access logs
- IP to city/country mapping database

Input – CloudFront access logs

The first two lines of each logfile will look as follows:

```
#Version: 1.0
#Fields: date time x-edge-location sc-bytes c-ip cs-method
   cs(Host) cs-uri-stem sc-status cs(Referer) cs(User-Agent)
      cs-uri-query cs(Cookie) x-edge-result-type
         x-edge-request-id x-host-header cs-protocol cs-bytes
```

After that, every line will depict one access, each field is separated by a tab character and that would look as follows:

```
2014-02-11  22:03:27  ATL50  611  24.98.201.202  GET
d20asd43wfx2.cloudfront.net  /public/assets/images/
ui-bg_1x400.png  404  http://www.minjar.com/index.html
Mozilla/5.0%2520(Windows%2520NT%25205.1)%2520AppleWebKit/537.36%2520
(KHTML,%2520like%2520Gecko)%2520Chrome/32.0.1700.107%2520Safari/537.36
- -
Error  1foSyTpksllq6WjX9RNV4c1XiCytd-FhwkyrbgOuCDEou7sm317CoQ==
asset1.minjarcdn.com  http  400
```

Among all the fields available in the logs, the following are the fields of concern for us:

- `Filename`
- `Edge Location`
- `Date`
- `Time`
- `IP`
- `HTTP status code`
- `Server to client bytes transferred`
- `Cache Hit/Miss/Error`

Input – IP to city/country mapping database

The logs have the IP address of the origin of request, but we need to get the insights per city and country. In order to convert IP to city or country, we need an IP to city/country mapping database. Many such free and paid databases are available.

You can use the MaxMind's developer version that is free. The database is named GeoLite2 and can be downloaded from `http://dev.maxmind.com/geoip/geoip2/geolite2`. MaxMind also provides you with the APIs in various languages to read this database. We will use the Java library provided by MaxMind to read the database file. You can read the documentation of their Java API at `http://maxmind.github.io/GeoIP2-java/`.

> Download the ZIP file having the JAR file and other dependencies from `http://geolite.maxmind.com/download/geoip/database/GeoLite2-City.mmdb.gz`.

Required libraries

The solution which we are going to create should have the following libraries in its class path:

- **Hadoop APIs**: The following libraries are required:
  - `hadoop-common-2.2.0.jar`
  - `hadoop-mapreduce-client-core-2.2.0.jar`

- **MaxMind APIs**: The following libraries are required:
  - `geoip2-0.7.0.jar`
  - `maxmind-db-0.3.1.jar`

- **MaxMind APIs' dependencies**: The following libraries are required:
  - `jackson-annotations-2.3.0.jar`
  - `jackson-core-2.3.0.jar`
  - `jackson-databind-2.3.0.jar`

- **Apache commons API**: The following libraries are required:
  - `commons-cli-1.2.jar`

Driver class implementation

You can refer to *Chapter 5, Programming Hadoop on Amazon EMR,* for details on what things are generally done in this class. This is basically a class where you create the Hadoop job and define the various configurations, including defining the Mapper and Reducer classes.

The structure of this class will be as follows:

```
public class LogAnalyzer extends Configured implements Tool {

  private static final String JOB_NAME = "CloudFront Log
    Analyzer";

  @Override
  public int run(String[] args) throws Exception {
  }

  public static void main(String[] args) throws Exception {
  }
}
```

You need to override the run method. First, within the run method, you should get the Configuration object and set the configuration which enables output to be compressed, as follows:

```
Configuration conf = getConf();

// set compression to be true by default
conf.setBoolean("mapred.output.compress", true);
```

Now, we also want the output to be directly ingested into a data store; hence, a true CSV output will help. So, in order to set the separator between the key and value in the output to be a comma character, the following configuration can be used:

```
conf.set("mapred.textoutputformat.separator", ",");
```

You need to pass on the MaxMind's mmdb database file to your job and make it available for each mapper task locally. For this, you can add this database file as a distributed cache. In addition to getting the input and output path(s), we also need to get the path to the database file. In order to get it from the arguments, we will use Apache CLI library, which is very simple to use, as shown in the following code:

```
Options options = new Options();
options.addOption("ipcitycountrymappingfile", true,
  "ipcitycountrymappingfile - IP to City Mapping File");
CommandLineParser parser = new PosixParser();
```

```
CommandLine cmd = parser.parse(options, args);
String ipcitycountrymappingfilePath =
    cmdgetOptionValue("ipcitycountrymappingfile");
```

Now, you can add this file to the distributed cache of your job. Using the
`DistributedCache` class, as shown in the following code, has been deprecated
in Hadoop 2.

```
DistributedCache.addCacheFile(new URI(argument), conf);
    // Deprecated
```

Instead of the `DistributedCache` class, use the `addCacheFile` method of job class,
as shown in the following code:

```
job.addCacheFile(new URI(ipcitycountrymappingfilePath));
```

Say along with analyzing logs on the basis of city and county, you also want to
analyze the logs on the basis of IPs, you would want different sets of outputs for each
of them. This can be achieved by using `MultipleOutputs` as discussed in *Chapter 9,
Hadoop Streaming and Advanced Hadoop Customizations*. Let's define two named
outputs, one for aggregating counts by city/country and the other for aggregating
by IP, as shown here:

```
MultipleOutputs.addNamedOutput(job, "detailsbycitycountry",
    TextOutputFormat.class, Text.class, Text.class);
MultipleOutputs.addNamedOutput(job, "detailsbyip",
  TextOutputFormat.class,
    Text.class, Text.class);
```

Now, empty `part-r-*****` files will be created, while `MultipleOutputs` is used
to emit the output.

The following statement makes sure that Hadoop emits the default output lazily,
that is, the output file will be created only when something is written to the context:

```
LazyOutputFormat.setOutputFormatClass(job,
    TextOutputFormat.class);
```

Other than this mentioned statement, you will need to provide the basic configurations
such as `Key` and `Value` classes and also at the end, you will need to call the
`job.waitForCompletion` method.

The following is the complete implementation of the driver class, which is
named `LogAnalyzer`:

```
public class LogAnalyzer extends Configured implements Tool {

    private static final String JOB_NAME = "CloudFront Log Analyzer";
```

```
@Override
public int run(String[] args) throws Exception {

  try {
    Configuration conf = getConf();
        conf.setBoolean("mapred.output.compress", true);
        conf.setInt("mapred.task.timeout", 0);
        conf.set("mapred.textoutputformat.separator", ",");

    Job job = Job.getInstance(conf);

    Options options = new Options();
    options.addOption("ipcitycountrymappingfile", true,
      "ipcitycountrymappingfile - IP to City Mapping File");
    CommandLineParser parser = new PosixParser();
    CommandLine cmd = parser.parse(options, args);
    String ipcitycountrymappingfilePath =
      cmdgetOptionValue("ipcitycountrymappingfile");

    if (ipcitycountrymappingfilePath!= null) {
      job.addCacheFile(new URI(ipcitycountrymappingfilePath));
    } else {
      throw new MissingArgumentException("Argument '"
          + "ipcitycountrymappingfile" + "' is required.");
    }

    job.setJarByClass(LogAnalyzer.class);
    job.setJobName(JOB_NAME);

    job.setMapperClass(LogAnalyzerMapper.class);
    job.setReducerClass(LogAnalyzerReducer.class);
    job.setOutputKeyClass(Text.class);
    job.setOutputValueClass(Text.class);
    job.setInputFormatClass(TextInputFormat.class);
    job.setOutputFormatClass(TextOutputFormat.class);
    job.setMapOutputValueClass(Text.class);
    job.setMapOutputKeyClass(Text.class);

    FileInputFormat.setInputPaths(job, args[0]);
    FileOutputFormat.setOutputPath(job, new Path(args[1]));

    // Define two named outputs, one for aggregating counts by
    // city/country and the other for aggregating by IP
```

```
        MultipleOutputs.addNamedOutput(job, "detailsbycitycountry",
          TextOutputFormat.class, Text.class, Text.class);
        MultipleOutputs.addNamedOutput(job, "detailsbyip",
          TextOutputFormat.class, Text.class, Text.class);
        LazyOutputFormat.setOutputFormatClass(job,
          TextOutputFormat.class);
        boolean success = job.waitForCompletion(true);
        return success ? 0 : 1;
      } catch (Exception e) {
        e.printStackTrace();
        return 1;
      }


    }


    public static void main(String[] args) throws Exception {

      if (args.length < 3) {
        System.out
            .println("Usage: LogAnalyzer <comma separated list of
              input directories>" +
                " <output dir> -ipcitymappingfile <path to mmdb
                  database>");
        System.exit(-1);
      }

      int result = ToolRunner.run(new LogAnalyzer(), args);
      System.exit(result);
    }
}
```

Mapper class implementation

The mapper processes each line in the input, finds the country to which the IP address belongs using MaxMind GeoIP2 API and the database. For each record in the logfile, the mapper outputs two key-value pairs, one for aggregation by city-country and the other for aggregation by IP.

In the setup method, you will need to get the IP to city-country mapping database file from the distributed cache and create an instance of the com.maxmind.geoip2.DatabaseReader class to be used in the map method implementation.

In the map method implementation, you can ignore the first two lines of each logfile, and as these two lines start with a hash character (#), they can easily be ignored. You then split each line on the tab character and extract the relevant fields.

Using the IP address which you would have extracted from the log record and the com.maxmind.geoip2.model.CityResponse class along with the DatabaseReader class, you would get the corresponding city and country. You can decide whether the access record is for a hit or a miss depending on the value of the xEdgeResultType column extracted from the log record.

Now, you will emit two sets of output from the mapper:

- **Set 1**: The following output is emitted:
    - Key = date, filename, scStatus, city, country, xEdgeLocation
    - Value = requestCount, hitCount, missCount, errorCount

- **Set 2**: The following output is emitted:
    - Key = date, filename, IP
    - Value = requestCount

You might want to emit different sets of key-value pairs as per your analysis requirements.

The following is the complete implementation of the Mapper class.

```
public class LogAnalyzerMapper extends Mapper<LongWritable, Text,
  Text, Text> {

  private Text outputValue = new Text("");
  private Text outputKey = new Text();
  DatabaseReader reader;

  /*
   * It reads the Maximind's database from Distributed Cache and
   creates
   * an instance of DatabaseReader for further use.
   */
  @Override
  public void setup(Context context) {

    URI ipCityMappingFile;
    try {
      ipCityMappingFile = context.getCacheFiles()[0];
      File database = new File(ipCityMappingFile.toString());

      reader = new DatabaseReader.Builder(database).build();
    } catch (IOException e) {
      e.printStackTrace();
```

```java
    }
  }

  @Override
  public void map(LongWritable key, Text value, Context context)
      throws IOException, InterruptedException {

    // The first 2 lines of each log file are info records
    // and hence should be ignored.
    // These lines start with the hash (#) character.
    if (value.toString().charAt(0) == '#') {
      return;
    }
    String[] valueRow = value.toString().split("\\t");

    /*
     * Fields: date time x-edge-location sc-bytes c-ip cs-method
     cs(Host)
     * cs-uri-stem sc-status cs(Referer) cs(User-Agent) cs-uri-
     query
     * cs(Cookie) x-edge-result-type x-edge-request-id
     */
    String date = valueRow[0];
    String xEdgeLocation = valueRow[2];
    String scBytes = valueRow[3];
    String cIP = valueRow[4];
    String csURIStem = valueRow[7];
    String scStatus = valueRow[8];
    String xEdgeResultType = valueRow[13];

    String city = "";
    String country = "";
    CityResponse response = null;
    try {
      response = reader.city(InetAddress.getByName(cIP));
      city = response.getCity().toString();
      country = response.getCountry().toString();
    } catch (GeoIp2Exception e) {
      e.printStackTrace();
      context.getCounter(Constants.CUSTOM_COUNTERS_GROUP_NAME,
          Constants.IP_TO_CITY_COUNTRY_MISS_COUNTER).increment(1);

    }

    // Output for Details_By Date_File_HTTPStatus_City_Country_
    EdgeLocation
```

```
        String filename = csURIStem.substring(csURIStem.lastIndexOf('/') +
    1);

        // Key = date, filename,  scStatus, city, country,
        xEdgeLocation
        outputKey.set(date + "," + filename + "," + scStatus + "," +
        city + ","
            + country + "," + xEdgeLocation);
        // Value = requestCount, hitCount, missCount, errorCount
        outputValue
            .set("1,"
                + (xEdgeResultType.toString().equals("Hit") ? "1,"
                    : "0,")
                + (xEdgeResultType.toString().equals("Miss") ? "1,"
                    : "0,")
                + ((!xEdgeResultType.toString().equals("Miss") &&
                !xEdgeResultType
                    .toString().equals("Hit")) ? "1," : "0,")
                + scBytes);
        context.write(outputKey, outputValue);

        context.getCounter("CUSTOM COUNTERS",
        "DETAILS BY CITY-COUNTRY").increment(1);

        // Output for Details_By_Date_File_IP
        outputKey.set(date + "," + filename + "," + cIP);
        outputValue.set("1");
        context.write(outputKey, outputValue);
        context.getCounter("CUSTOM COUNTERS",
        "DETAILS BY IP").increment(1);
    }

}
```

Reducer class implementation

In the Reducer class, you will need to initialize a MultipleOutputs instance and
use it to emit both kinds of aggregated results, that is, aggregation by city-country
and aggregation by IP. This initialization has to be done in the setup method and do
not forget to override the cleanup method as well and close the MultipleOutputs
instance here.

In the `reduce` method implementation, you will need to split the key's string value on a comma character and according to the split array size, you can decide that is it details by city-country or details by IP.

The following is a complete implementation of the `Reducer` class:

```
public class LogAnalyzerReducer extends Reducer<Text, Text, Text,
  Text> {

  private Text outputValue = new Text("");

  // Using MultipleOutputs to output data in different folders.
  private MultipleOutputs<Text, Text> multipleOutputs;

  @Override
  protected void setup(Context context) throws IOException,
      InterruptedException {

    super.setup(context);
    multipleOutputs = new MultipleOutputs<Text, Text>(context);
  }

  @Override
  protected void reduce(Text key, Iterable<Text> values, Context
    context)
      throws IOException, InterruptedException {

    Iterator<Text> iterator = values.iterator();
    Integer requestCount = 0;
    Integer missCount = 0;
    Integer hitCount = 0;
    Integer errCount = 0;
    Integer bytesTransferred = 0;
    String[] keyRows = key.toString().split(",");
    if (keyRows.length == 6) { // DETAILS_BY_CITY_COUNTRY data
      while (iterator.hasNext()) {
        Text value = iterator.next();
        String[] rows = value.toString().split(",");
        requestCount += Integer.parseInt(rows[0]);
        hitCount += Integer.parseInt(rows[1]);
        missCount += Integer.parseInt(rows[2]);
        errCount += Integer.parseInt(rows[3]);
        bytesTransferred += Integer.parseInt(rows[4]);
      }
```

```
          outputValue.set(requestCount + "," + hitCount + "," +
      missCount + "," + errCount + "," + bytesTransferred);
          multipleOutputs.write("detailsbycitycountry", key, outputValue,
            "detailsbycitycountry" + File.separator + "part");
        } else if (keyRows.length == 3) { // DETAILS_BY_IP data
          while (iterator.hasNext()) {
            iterator.next();
            requestCount++;
          }
          outputValue.set(requestCount + "");
          multipleOutputs.write("detailsbyip", key, outputValue,
            "detailsbyip" + File.separator + "part");
        }
      }

    @Override
    protected void cleanup(Context context) throws IOException,
        InterruptedException {

      multipleOutputs.close();
    }
  }
```

Testing the solution locally

You can build the JAR file for the above solution as explained in *Chapter 5, Programming Hadoop on Amazon EMR*, and then you will need to make sure that your local Hadoop configuration has details about the compression codec or not, as you would have noticed we are setting `compression` to `true`.

You can see a file named `mapred-site.xml.template` or `mapred-site.xml` in your local copy of Hadoop at `/<base-path>/hadoop-2.2.0/etc/hadoop`. If it is the `.template` file, then remove this `.template` suffix and add the following section in the XML file:

```xml
<?xml version="1.0" encoding="UTF-8"?>
<configuration>
    <property>
        <name>mapred.output.compression.codec</name>
        <value>org.apache.hadoop.io.compress.GzipCodec</value>
    </property>
</configuration>
```

Now, you can test this locally by executing the following command:

```
/<base-path>/hadoop-2.2.0/bin/hadoop jar /<jar- directory
>/cloudfront_log_analyzer.jar <input-file-or- directory -path>
<output-directory-path> -ipcitymappingfile /< geolite-directory
>/GeoLite2-City.mmdb
```

On successful completion of the job, you will see two directories in the `output` folder, namely, `detailsbycitycountry` and `detailsbyip`. The output files within them should be gzipped.

Executing the solution on EMR

You should upload the input logfiles to S3 or use your own CloudFront access logs location on S3 as an input. You should also upload the `cloudfront_log_analyzer. jar` file and the `mmdb` database file to S3.

Now, using the CLI client tool, as described in *Chapter 8, Amazon EMR – Command-line Interface Client,* you will first need to launch a cluster and then add the Job Step to it, using the following command:

```
ruby elastic-mapreduce --create --alive --name "CloudFront Log Analysis"
\
--ami-version 3.0.4 \
--master-instance-type m1.medium --slave-instance-type m1.medium \
--num-instances 1
```

This command will give you a Job Flow ID.

Next, you need to add the Job Step for the log analysis. You can do that using the following command:

```
ruby elastic-mapreduce --jobflow <jobFloeId> \
--jar s3://learning-bigdata/LogAnalyzer/bin/
cloudfront_log_analyzer.jar \
--args s3://learning-bigdata/LogAnalyzer/input/cloudfront_logs/,
s3://learning-bigdata/LogAnalyzer/output/1/ \
--args -ipcitymappingfile, s3://learning-
bigdata/LogAnalyzer/input/GeoLite2-City.mmdb \
--step-name "LogAnalyzer"
```

After successful completion of the Job Step, you can download the output and get ready to ingest data into a data store to be consumed by a visualization tool.

Output ingestion to a data store

As discussed earlier, we are going to use MySQL. In any MySQL server, either local or remote, create two tables, `details_by_city_country` and `details_by_ip`. Let's just focus on the `details_by_city_country` table. In accordance with the output from our reducer, you can create it using the following command:

```
CREATE TABLE details_by_city_country (

date date NOT NULL,

filename varchar(100) NOT NULL,

http_status_code integer NOT NULL,

city varchar(100) NOT NULL,

country varchar(100) NOT NULL,

edge_location varchar(10) NOT NULL,

request_count BIGINT NOT NULL,

hit_count BIGINT NOT NULL,

miss_count BIGINT NOT NULL,

error_count BIGINT NOT NULL,

bytes_transferred BIGINT NOT NULL

);
```

You should combine all the output in `<output-directory-path>/detailsbycitycountry/` using the following command:

```
zcat output-directory-path>/detailsbycitycountry/part-r-* >
detailsbycitycountry.csv
```

Now, you can import it to MySQL using the `LOAD DATA LOCAL INFILE` command of MySQL.

Similarly, you can import data to MySQL for the `details_by_ip` table.

You are now ready to use any visualization tool to create graphs and charts by connecting to this data store.

Using a visualization tool – Tableau Desktop

We chose Tableau Desktop as our visualization tool because it is very simple to install and use. In order to use this tool, you need to have either Windows or Mac as it isn't available currently for any Linux distributions.

Setting up Tableau Desktop

Get the executable/installer for Tableau Desktop from `http://www.tableausoftware.com/products/desktop/download`.

After the completion of download, execute the installer and follow the instructions to complete the setup.

As we are going to connect to MySQL, its connector also needs to be installed. You can go to `http://www.tableausoftware.com/support/drivers` and download and install the correct driver. If you are using any other data store instead of MySQL, you can install the relevant driver.

Creating a new worksheet and connecting to the data store

The following steps create a new worksheet and connect to MySQL:

1. Start the Tableau Desktop program and go to **File | New**.

2. Click on either **Data | Connect to Data** or click on **Connect to Data** on the left-hand side section, as shown in the following screenshot:

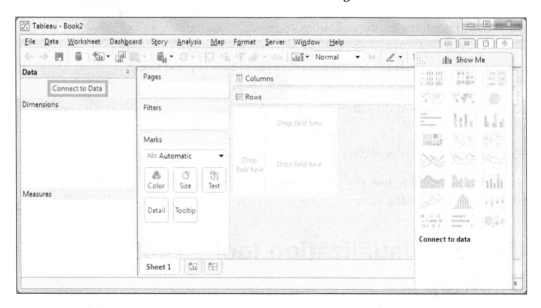

3. Select **MySQL** from the left-hand side section and key in your MySQL
   server's details and click on **Connect**:

4. Select the **cloudfront_log_analysis** option from the **Database** dropdown and
   click on **Go to Worksheet**, as shown in the following screenshot:

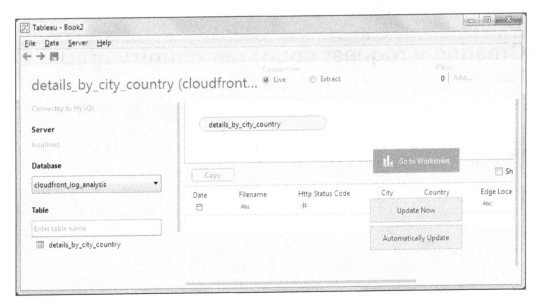

This will take you to a screen, as shown in the following screenshot:

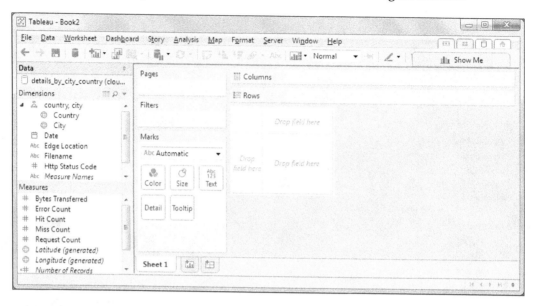

As you can see, Tableau automatically decides which columns/fields can be the dimensions and which can be the measures. Dimensions generally form the rows and measures are taken to be part of columns while creating graphs and tabular charts.

Creating a request count per country graph

The following steps will create a request count per country graph:

1. Drag **Country** from the **Dimensions** section and drop it into the **Rows** section on the right-hand side pane.

2. Similarly, drag **Request Count** from the **Measures** section and drop it into the **Columns** section on the right-hand side pane.

3. You can see the horizontal bar graph, as shown in the following screenshot:

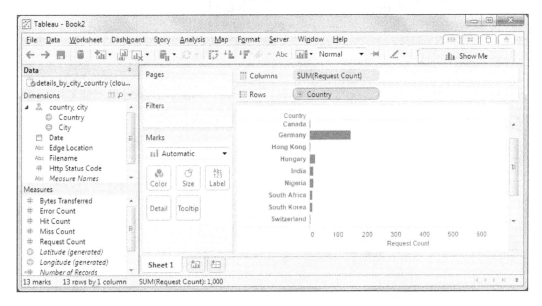

That's all you need to do. Now, if you want to see an ordered list of values, you can click on the right-hand side of the **Country** label in the **Rows** section and click on **Sort...**, as shown in the following screenshot:

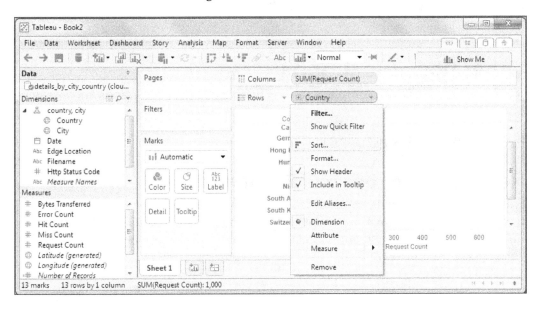

You will get a popup where you should select **Descending** and click on **OK**. Now, you should see the results with the country with the highest number of request counts at the top, as shown in the following screenshot:

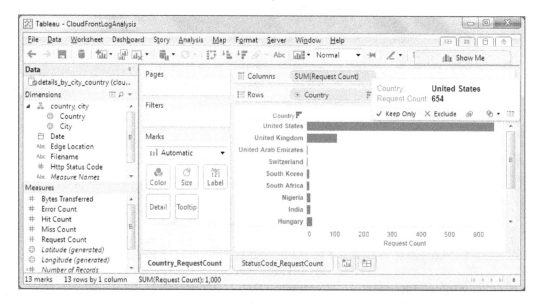

If you want different types of graphs and charts, you can click on **Show Me** on the top-right corner and select among multiple choices ranging from pie charts to tree maps.

Other possible graphs

Similar to the preceding example, you can create many possible graphs and charts as per your requirements.

The following sections provide a few more examples.

Request count per HTTP status code

Similar to creating visualization for request count per country, you can also create the visualization to know the request count per HTTP status code. This bar chart can be useful in finding out the number of erroneous requests and whether their counts are under considerable limits or not.

The following screenshot shows the request count per HTTP status code:

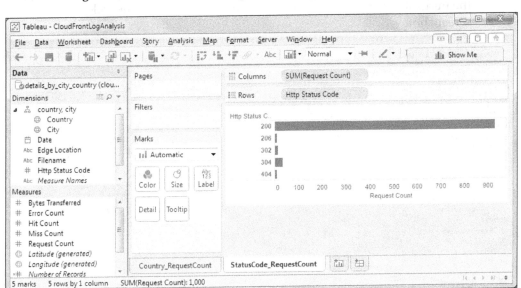

Request count per edge location

To obtain a request count per edge location, perform the following steps:

1. Let's create a pie chart for the request counts served per edge location. Drag **Edge Location** from the **Dimensions** section and drop it into the **Rows** section on the right-hand side pane.

2. Similarly, drag **Request Count** from the **Measures** section and drop it into the **Columns** section on the right-hand side pane.

3. Now, click on **Show Me** in the top-right corner and select **piechart** among the multiple choices. The output should be as shown in the following screenshot:

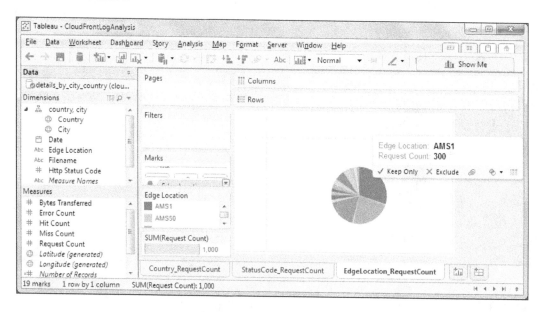

Bytes transferred per country

Let's create a packed bubbles visual for the bytes transferred per country:

1. Drag **Country** from the **Dimensions** section and drop it into the **Rows** section on the right-hand side pane.

2. Similarly, drag **Bytes Transferred** from the **Measures** section and drop it into the **Columns** section on the right-hand side pane.

3. Now, click on **Show Me** in the top-right corner and select **packed bubbles** among the multiple choices.

4. The output should be as shown in the following screenshot:

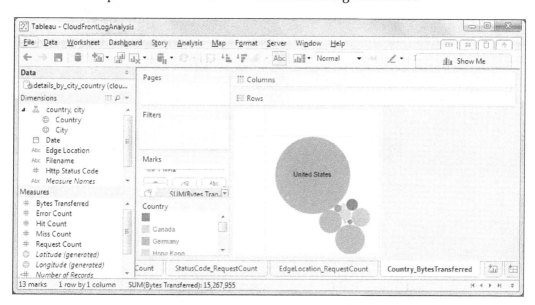

You can play around and create more than one view per page and add filters on top of the results.

Summary

In this chapter, we leveraged what we have learned in this book and created a real-world solution of getting business insights from CloudFront logs. Using this visual data, the business might want to focus more on certain areas in the world from where it receives maximum hits, and at the same time, some businesses might use it to find out the areas where they need to work on marketing and improve upon the hits from those areas.

We hope that by following this book, you have become familiar with the opportunities that lie in Big Data processing and have learned the two major technologies involved with it: Hadoop MapReduce and Amazon ElasticMapReduce. By now, you should have become familiar with the MapReduce paradigm that enables massively distributed processing. You should also be comfortable now in creating solutions and executing them on EMR clusters.

You should now try out creating solutions using Hadoop for various business problems such as creating a movie recommendation engine or market basket analysis.

Hadoop as well as EMR are improving continuously. Follow their official pages online at `http://hadoop.apache.org` and `http://aws.amazon.com/elasticmapreduce/` and keep yourself updated.

Index

Tez 68
tools, AWS 113
troubleshooting, EMR cluster 134

U

use case definition 185
User Defined Functions (UDFs) 68

V

visualization tool
  using 199

W

web console (AWS management console)
  about 73
  used, for accessing AWS EMR service 125
WebService API
  about 73
  used, for accessing AWS EMR service 126
websites
  hosting, on master node 136, 137

word count example, streaming
  about 164
  mapper 164
  reducer 165, 166
write method, MultipleOutputs
    class 181, 182

Y

YARN, Apache Hadoop
  about 57, 64, 65
  ApplicationMaster (AM) 66
  benefits 67
  container 67
  entities 66
  NodeManager 66
  ResourceManager (RM) 66
  working 65

Z

ZooKeeper 68

Thank you for buying
Learning Big Data with Amazon Elastic MapReduce

About Packt Publishing

Packt, pronounced 'packed', published its first book "Mastering phpMyAdmin for Effective MySQL Management" in April 2004 and subsequently continued to specialize in publishing highly focused books on specific technologies and solutions.

Our books and publications share the experiences of your fellow IT professionals in adapting and customizing today's systems, applications, and frameworks. Our solution based books give you the knowledge and power to customize the software and technologies you're using to get the job done. Packt books are more specific and less general than the IT books you have seen in the past. Our unique business model allows us to bring you more focused information, giving you more of what you need to know, and less of what you don't.

Packt is a modern, yet unique publishing company, which focuses on producing quality, cutting-edge books for communities of developers, administrators, and newbies alike. For more information, please visit our website: www.packtpub.com.

About Packt Enterprise

In 2010, Packt launched two new brands, Packt Enterprise and Packt Open Source, in order to continue its focus on specialization. This book is part of the Packt Enterprise brand, home to books published on enterprise software – software created by major vendors, including (but not limited to) IBM, Microsoft and Oracle, often for use in other corporations. Its titles will offer information relevant to a range of users of this software, including administrators, developers, architects, and end users.

Writing for Packt

We welcome all inquiries from people who are interested in authoring. Book proposals should be sent to author@packtpub.com. If your book idea is still at an early stage and you would like to discuss it first before writing a formal book proposal, contact us; one of our commissioning editors will get in touch with you.

We're not just looking for published authors; if you have strong technical skills but no writing experience, our experienced editors can help you develop a writing career, or simply get some additional reward for your expertise.

Programming MapReduce with Scalding

ISBN: 978-1-78328-701-7   Paperback: 148 pages

A practical guide to designing, testing, and implementing complex MapReduce applications in Scala

1. Develop MapReduce applications using a functional development language in a lightweight, high-performance, and testable way.

2. Recognize the Scalding capabilities to communicate with external data stores and perform machine learning operations.

Instant MapReduce Patterns – Hadoop Essentials How-to

ISBN: 978-1-78216-770-9   Paperback: 60 pages

Practical recipes to write your own MapReduce solution patterns for Hadoop programs

1. Learn something new in an Instant! A short, fast, focused guide delivering immediate results.

2. Learn how to install, configure, and run Hadoop jobs.

3. Seven recipes, each describing a particular style of the MapReduce program to give you a good understanding of how to program with MapReduce.

Please check **www.PacktPub.com** for information on our titles

Hadoop MapReduce Cookbook

ISBN: 978-1-84951-728-7   Paperback: 300 pages

Recipes for analyzing large and complex datasets with Hadoop MapReduce

1. Learn to process large and complex datasets, starting simply, then diving in deep.

2. Solve complex Big Data problems such as classifications, finding relationships, online marketing, and recommendations.

3. More than 50 Hadoop MapReduce recipes, presented in a simple and straightforward manner, with step-by-step instructions and real world examples.

Big Data Analytics with R and Hadoop

ISBN: 978-1-78216-328-2   Paperback: 238 pages

Set up an integrated infrastructure of R and Hadoop to turn your data analytics into Big Data analytics

1. Write Hadoop MapReduce within R.

2. Learn data analytics with R and the Hadoop platform.

3. Handle HDFS data within R.

4. Understand Hadoop streaming with R.

Please check **www.PacktPub.com** for information on our titles

www.ingramcontent.com/pod-product-compliance
Lightning Source LLC
Chambersburg PA
CBHW082118070326
40690CB00049B/3611